WEDNESDAYS WITH AVROM

INSIGHTFUL LESSONS FROM A REMARKABLE MAN

JARED DUNKIN

WEDNESDAYS WITH AVROM

Insightful Lessons From A Remarkable Man

Published by Mensch Press

Copyright © 2022 by Jared Dunkin

ISBN: 979-8-9861079-1-2

Library of Congress Control Number: 2022936697

All photos that accompany chapters are from either Unsplash or Pexels and are used under their licenses for commercial works.

Author info:

Publisher: themenschpress.com
Book: wednesdayswithavrom.com
Email: wednesdayswithavrom@gmail.com

100% of profits go to charity, Yad Yehuda of Greater Washington

"A prisoner cannot release himself from the prison he is in."

—Talmud, Berachot 5b

To Avrom Landesman, my teacher, mentor, and friend, who "released" me from my misconceptions and led me on a path of purpose, meaning, and significance.

CONTENTS

INTRODUCTION

Twenty-five years ago, I was deeply touched by the book *Tuesdays with Morrie*. I was in college at the time and was determined to find my Morrie.

Many years later, I met Avrom. He is the wisest, smartest, humblest, happiest, kindest, and funniest person I know. He has touched the lives of many thousands of people around the world and certainly mine.

After a health scare at age 85 during the Covid pandemic, I realized I must grab every moment I can with him. Over the course of a year, my wife and I visited him each Wednesday. She brought him two soups and baked goods, while I brought him the challenges and concerns of how to be a good husband, father, leader, and person.

Mel Brooks, 95 years old, ends his autobiography, *All About Me!* stating, "I'm also proud to say that I have made people laugh for a living, and whether or not you'll allow me to, I'm going to brag – I can honestly say, I've done it as well as anybody. I started in 1938 as a street-corner comic in Brooklyn, and I'm still doing it... just on more well-known street corners."

Avrom grew up on the same street-corner as Mr. Brooks. On Avrom's "new" street corner, he has used laughter to bring joy to thousands and shared his human greatness and wisdom to teach scores of people how to live meaningful, purposeful, and contributive lives.

Avrom has deep life experience, broad knowledge, and overflowing care for all. His wisdom is the ability to translate all this to a specific individual at a specific time in a way that the person can relate.

This short book, written during visiting Avrom for a full year, is a window into how he helped me as I grappled with finding purpose, becoming a more compassionate leader, and being a mensch.

I am confident that Avrom's wisdom will change your life as much as it has changed mine. And, when you are 95, may you be able to say as boldly as Mr. Brooks (and Avrom), "I've done it as well as anybody."

PART 1:
FINDING PURPOSE

CHAPTER 1 – FULFILLMENT

THE TALMUD asks, "When does a man have joy?" One sage teaches it is when he experiences the fulfillment of knowing when and how to address each issue or difficult question in life.

Every Wednesday afternoon, I have the tremendous privilege of meeting with Avrom, an 85-year-old giant of a man. Avrom is certainly the wisest, smartest, humblest, happiest, kindest, and funniest person I know. He has touched the lives of many thousands of people around the world and certainly has had an unbelievable impact on my life. We joke that although the visits are on Wednesdays it is our *Tuesdays with Morrie* moments.

Every child knows that mining under the surface is where the gems will be found. Yet, we forget this in our busy lives and miss much of what life has to teach us. Anyone who meets Avrom immediately picks up that he is a rare gem who not only shines but magically makes anyone who comes into contact with him radiate.

Here are a couple of stories Avrom shared with me on defining and achieving fulfillment in life.

Nuance.

Avrom told me that the first time he went to the Guggenheim Museum in NYC was when he was a teen. There was an exhibit of a large piece of art that was seemingly painted black. A sign said that you needed to stand back and stare at the upper left corner for a few minutes and a series of circles would appear. After seeing the circles, he said to himself, "Maybe this will be a great way to make a living – selling nuance." He attended Harvard Law School and made a living in selling the greatest nuance of all – the law.

Brains, Money, and Turning Hunches into Action.

In the 1960s, Avrom started a successful and interesting journey in government eventually becoming a top lawyer for the U.S. Department of Energy. As a father of young children, he was heavily involved in the community and schools. Avrom was one of the youngest members of the board of directors of the school and noticed that the board was comprised of brilliant doctors and lawyers as well as wealthy businesspeople who largely were self-made real estate developers. Avrom noticed there was not necessarily a correlation between brains and money. The real estate moguls' success was their ability to turn a hunch into action and push forward with relentless determination.

Avrom realized at a young age that money is important and having lots of it allowed real estate moguls to be extremely charitable, but chasing wealth was not the route for him in life. Rather, he sought a career that was intellectually challenging, fulfilling, and meaningful.

Avrom understood that confusion arises from the perception of choice – we experience more clarity by reducing options and pursuing our defined mission. While nuance is a great way to make a living, it is not a great way to live life. This distinction is a subtle one. Like the real estate moguls, Avrom had a hunch what a fulfilling career should be, acted on it, and with patient determination achieved it. But instead of piles of money, he found; fulfillment!

There is no theory that can truly explain fulfillment. It starts as a hunch and is achieved by action. No matter where you are in life it is not too late to stand back and stare at the upper left corner of your life and focus on your definition of fulfillment. The circles and connections will appear – your job is to know the treasure is there, be present enough to sense what will bring fulfillment to you, and act when you receive the hunch.

CHAPTER 2 – WHERE ARE YOU?

"Life is a journey to be experienced, not a problem to be solved." – Winnie the Pooh

LIFE IS HArd to navigate by ourselves. It is for this reason we need an avuncular figure who has the experiences and memories of a lifetime to help us put our lives in context. These wise individuals understand success is not defined by money or Facebook likes, but, rather, by the joy in living meaningfully and experiencing all life's grandeur. It is easy to wait for life to happen to us as we seek achievements such as finishing school, getting married, entering the workforce, or attaining some perceived professional success. We spend much of our lives investing in what we will become rather than in enjoying the experiences of the moment.

At a young age Avrom left home in Pennsylvania to live with his grandmother in Brooklyn so that he could advance his studies. After years of intense learning, he attended college in New York. To satisfy his unrelenting curiosity, Avrom sought as broad a liberal arts education as possible and formed a close relationship with each of his professors.

One by one Avrom's professors called him into their office to instruct him on what he should do with his life. First, it was his history professor, "Avrom, you have a terrific understanding of the inter-relationship of world events, history is the most important thing in the world, and you must devote your entire life to mastering it." Next, it was his political science professor, "Avrom, you have a brilliant mastery of people and politics, there is nothing more important to study, forget everything else and focus all your energy on it." Each professor repeated a similar message to Avrom, even the physical education teacher.

Avrom reflected on their comments and realized, "They can't all be right, I am interested in all these topics and more." He graciously thanked his professors and resolved to continuously kindle his broad curiosity and not put all his attention on one thing. More importantly, Avrom realized there are many aspects to a healthy life, including professional, personal, spiritual, and physical. He intuited that if he could nourish all these aspects his life would be richer and more meaningful.

But how do we do this? Society bombards us with the message that we must be "all in" work. However, if you have nothing but work on your mind, you become one-dimensional, as whatever you are doing will be clouded by thinking of work. On the other hand, if you try to be in too many places at once you are actually nowhere. As the Talmud teaches, "When you grasp for everything, you end up grasping for nothing." And to make matters even more challenging, we have a little device in our pockets whose entire purpose is to steal our attention.

Avrom changed my life by helping me understand the broader context of my life's journey and how each day is a series of transitions between my spiritual, professional, physical, and personal life. Each of these areas need to be nourished. And the secret is, because you are where your mind is, to be "all in" whatever you are doing. "All in" requires being mindful, and fully engaged in the activity you are pursuing at the present moment. That is, 100 percent on work when at work, 100 percent on family when with family, and 100 percent engaged in exercise when exercising. And when we get this transition right, we create a virtuous cycle of good as each part of our lives enhances and strengthens the other. We then appreciate and experience the tremendous power of each moment of each day of our life.

CHAPTER 3 – IT'S (NOT) ALL RELATIVE...

H.L. Mᴇɴᴄᴋᴇɴ quipped that the test of wealth is any income that is at least one hundred dollars more a year than the income of one's wife's sister's husband. Unfortunately, for many, wealth is not defined in absolute terms but in rather 'relative' ones.

Avrom taught me to view wealth as being happy and content with one's situation as measured in terms of contribution.

In 1986, Avrom was in his early 50s and at the peak of his career – he had just orchestrated a massive civil settlement with big oil companies, discussed in later chapters. However, the winds had changed in the Reagan administration in favor of big oil companies. And, to the pleasure of the administration, Avrom agreed to an early retirement from the government.

Avrom was at a crossroads and needed to make a career decision. He was courted with lucrative offers by prestigious oil companies and law firms. In addition, he was aware of the need for his talents in communal matters. He decided to establish a private consulting practice where he could effectively assist big oil companies, provide mediation services, and still have time to work on communal issues. To accomplish this, Avrom gave up a significant amount of money and professional prestige. And his decision proved successful; he earned sufficiently to cover his needs and enjoyed the freedom he had to decide with whom he wanted to work and devote his energy.

Over the next 30 years, Avrom was instrumental in establishing three schools (elementary, high school, and yeshiva), supporting multiple charitable and religious institutions, and providing uncountable hours of counseling and teaching. He has had an incalculable impact on the lives of so many people and has led a rich, fulfilling life.

Avrom's happiness stems from his ability to see the big picture and his awareness of how to best utilize his unique skill sets. Throughout the years he has been able to integrate his personal needs and interests with his intellectual and religious pursuits.

Here's the lesson – there are many factors that contribute to one's happiness. The key is to know what drives you, visualize what is important to you, and appreciate that each person has his or her unique path in the world. This will result in a contribution that only you can make (without any reference to your wife's sister's husband). And lastly, recognize that our lives are not static, and desires, drives and priorities can shift. Changing gears is not only okay, but it often will lead to a richer and more complete life experience.

CHAPTER 4 – THE STORIES WE TELL...

THE BIGGEST obstacle to being present in the moment and enjoying the richness of life is the fixation we have with the storylines swirling in our minds. Stories can be motivating, seductive, helpful, or sometimes even necessary. But the ones I specifically refer to here are the unhelpful stories we tell ourselves. These stories relate to negative events from our past, concerns about our future, and the discomfort or anxiety we may feel about our present situation that prevents us from simply being able to inhabit and enjoy the present.

Over the past 60 years, Avrom has counseled thousands of people on various aspects of life. A common theme he notices revolves around replaying, regretting, and rewriting the script of one's life; "I could have…," "if only I would have…," or "maybe it's not too late to…."

Avrom recalls the following story he heard as a child:

A well-dressed young man is travelling on a horse-drawn coach. There is a middle-aged man in the coach sitting opposite him, intently reading his newspaper. Once the trip starts, the young man says to the older man, "Excuse me, sir, can you tell me what time it is?" The older man ignores him entirely and keeps reading his paper. A few minutes later, the younger man clears his throat and again says, "Excuse me, sir, can you tell me what time it is?" Again, the man ignores his question. Finally, the young man says, "Sir, is it really so difficult to tell me what time it is?" The older man puts down his paper and says, "Actually, it is no trouble at all to tell you the time. But, if I did, we would start a conversation. I would ask you your destination and you would ask me mine. It would turn out we're going to the same city which happens to be where I live. I would feel compelled to invite you to visit my home. You would accept my invitation. When you arrive, you would notice my young and beautiful daughter. She would be impressed by you. You would ask her for a date. She would agree. You would like each other, fall in love, and get married. And I'll be damned to get a son-in-law who doesn't even own a watch!"

It appears the older man was telling himself a ludicrous story triggered by a harmless question, "What time is it?" But, if we are honest with ourselves, don't we all do this as well? We ruminate over such stories, creating stress, negative energy and, worst of all, diverting our (and sometimes others') attention from the significance and unlimited possibilities of the moment.

People seek Avrom's counsel for the wisdom, kindness, and deep caring he bestows. When giving guidance he considers each person's unique situation and has benefited many people simply by reframing their impulse to say, "I could have…," "if only I would have…," or "maybe it's not too late…."

I asked him how he does it. He told me that first, he just listens to the person and calms them down. This is important in order to drop the destructive storylines. When people tell him that they could have been something different or should have married the other person, he listens, empathizes, and validates (which many times is all the person needs). He then might make a joke to help them realize the silliness of the storyline, "I always wanted to be a major league baseball shortstop, but I am short and have no athletic ability."

Next, once the mind is settled, Avrom moves to action, "Let's figure out how we can help you find meaning in your life. Keep in mind we need to be practical and avoid radical decisions." Switching from accounting to brain surgery may be a noble pursuit but, for a 50-year-old, it is likely not practical – it would take at least 10 years of schooling and significant lost income during that time, and, for someone with a spouse and children, mortgage, and school fees must be considered. Avrom explains the negative repercussions that such radical changes may yield.

Lastly, Avrom teaches them that all we can really control in life is our perspective. There is meaning and beauty all around us if we just open our eyes to see it. We may think there are seemingly more important or bigger things we should be doing, but we need to be mindful of our existing responsibilities in this world. He counsels that there is nothing more valuable or meaningful than the loved ones around us.

These principles can be applied to many of our struggles. Next time you get lost in a storyline or start worrying about something you should have done or failed to do, try to slow down, and don't make any radical decisions. Learn to appreciate your responsibilities and the many blessings you have. And when you are on the subway and a nice young man asks for the time, don't think twice about it, just tell him the time. He may even surprise you and respond that he is on his way to pick up his new watch!

CHAPTER 5 – REALLY NO ONE...

L IKE MOST people, I have been persuaded by the self-help industry that there is a magical 'one thing' solution for each challenge I encounter. I am guilty of being susceptible to this thinking as I have always so desperately wanted the easy fix.

"Avrom, I have a problem at work involving competing interests on an initiative; I need your help figuring out the best way forward." I then earnestly described the delicate situation with which I was confronted. "Jared, let me tell you a story; growing up my little sister was the youngest child by nine years. She was the darling and princess of the family. When she was still a little girl, someone asked her which parent she liked best. Without missing a beat, she cleverly said, I like my mother best and my father better."

Avrom went on to explain how a single theory to describe the fundamental forces of nature eluded Einstein his entire life. He then laughed and asked me, "Mirror, mirror on the wall, who is the fairest of them all?"

"Like Einstein and Snow White, the premise that there is a single 'best of everything' reflects a common misunderstanding. It is not true that there is a 'universal' 'first,' 'single,' or 'best.'" Avrom's analysis has been reinforced over the years as he helped thousands of people. Many of them, while searching for the single solution to their problems, exhibited anxiety and frustration. "People mistakenly expend a lot of effort and energy looking for the single solution to happiness in life, when, in fact, there is no such thing."

Avrom elaborated on this point, "There is a single person to whom a married person should direct their love, but there is not a single child that a parent should love best. There is not a single ideal design for a house, many types of houses work well. There is not a single best design for a bridge, it depends on type of traffic, length of bridge, road to which bridge attaches, etc. There is not a single best form of government, it depends on society, whether need for monarchial figure, level of trust for peers to govern, etc. Similarly, there is not a single way to analyze, to teach, to believe, to love, to paint, to dress, etc."

"But Avrom, aren't there some areas where there is really just 'one thing'?" Avrom expounded that perhaps the foundations of religion influenced our craving for unitary theories for everything else. "Jared, this may be true in religion and some fields, but not true universally. It is important you question the premise."

Here's the lesson – in most areas of life there is not a single quick fix, one thing to do, best choice, or right decision. Life is messy. There are usually a number of answers which may all be of equal value. The takeaway is you won't solve your problem if you start with the assumption that there is a single answer. Consider all the possible solutions and then decide whether there is one answer that is overwhelmingly more applicable than the others.

Of course, there is the 'magical one thing' that is always certain – if someone tells you their advice is the best, only, single thing, run away!

CHAPTER 6 – COMING TOGETHER...

IN THE CORPORATE world, there is a popular and healthy trend of bringing your whole self to work. Avrom figured this out over 75 years ago.

When Avrom was a young child, his family spent summers at Lake Erie. The kids would spend every day at the beach, swimming and watching small fishing boats leave from the several wharfs. Most boats left in the evening and fished all night, returning in early morning with their catches.

Spending many hours gazing at the lake, Avrom noticed that if one looks at the horizon, it is not possible to tell where the water ends, and the sky begins. The two just come together as though there was a continuum.

Avrom often tried to see if he could detect a demarcation line, perhaps at certain times of the day or perhaps during varying water patterns, but he could not find the line of separation.

When Avrom was older, and engaged in religious studies, he realized that there was a profound symbol to his puzzle. That is, although there is a vast distance between the Earth and Heaven, there is a point – like the horizon – where they come together and merge.

Man has a spiritual life and a material life, and we must figure out how they should be merged.

Here's the lesson – the point of intersection is impossible to identify because it is impossible to compartmentalize the two. Effectiveness at work requires many inputs – energy, experience, time, focus, and motivation. Our outer work persona, comprised of these inputs, is nourished by our inner personal being and vice versa. The notion of work life balance is misleading because it suggests a tension. Successful integration of our outer work persona and inner being is achieved through harmony. Just as with the horizon, there is not a single point of intersection between the two but rather a seamless bond that fuses the one to the other.

CHAPTER 7 – THIS IS ABSURD...

SHANE SMITH, the founder of VICE Media, started the company with a mission to expose the "absurdity of the modern condition." For instance, we have endless traffic jams, yet we continue to build more cars; one might ask, "Who is in charge?"

During a visit to Israel in 1980, Avrom and several friends took a side trip to Egypt. Not far from Cairo a tour guide took them to see a temple built during the Fifth Dynasty (3,000-4,000 years ago) for Ra, the ancient Egyptian deity of the sun. It was a magnificent site, with two rows of very tall and wide marble pillars in perfect symmetry. The guide explained that there is no marble in the area of the temple, and it had to be transported from several hundred miles away.

Avrom was amazed as he contemplated how difficult it must have been to move these huge marble pillars hundreds of miles, especially at a time when only primitive wheels and tools were available. He mused to the guide that obviously only many thousands of slaves could have accomplished such a feat. However, the government guide insisted that many farmers, idle during much of the year in the desert, volunteered out of deep religious conviction, to participate in this phenomenal project. It was fairly evident that the government did not want modern tourist to believe that, even in ancient times, Egypt ever had slavery.

Like Shane, Avrom left Egypt wondering who was in charge. Thousands of years ago, Pharaohs ruled the land and had absolute power. At their personal whim, however ridiculous it might have been, vast expenditures and resources were devoted to their chosen projects. With no check on the Pharaoh's power, people were unable to ask what benefit would come from this project or even simply what its purpose was.

Modern democracy has seemingly fixed the danger of having an absolute political leader, especially one who convinces people that a higher Divine power guides their actions and sanctions them. We still haven't resolved for absurdity. It has been over 3,000 years since the temple was built for Ra and it has been deeply researched and studied. Applying our modern eyes, it may seem absurd, but was it at the time?

If we are honest, perhaps we will become aware that we live in the midst of continuous absurdity as well. Shane found, "A lot of what happens in the world is full-on crazy and doesn't get reported on."

On an individual level, there may be little we can do about most absurdity, but we can help ourselves. And it just starts with taking a step back to identify the absurdities in our own lives and accepting that we are in charge. Some of them we can change. The others? …. Well, we should just laugh.

CHAPTER 8 – GOING TOO FAR...

"Never give in—never, never, never, never, in nothing great or small, large or petty, never give in except to convictions of honour and good sense." Winston Churchill.

THE JOHN F. Kennedy Center for the Performing Arts in Washington, D.C., commonly known as the Kennedy Center, opened in 1971 and its success is evidenced by its 50th anniversary celebration. This milestone reminded Avrom of an eye-opening incident.

Avrom had attended an exceptionally moving symphony performance at the Kennedy Center and wanted to share his excitement. He mentioned it to a senior policy advisor with a doctorate in Economics with whom he worked at the Department of Commerce. He expressed his appreciation of the Kennedy Center as a place to enjoy excellent entertainment. The gentleman adamantly replied, "As a matter of principle, I will never set foot in that place!" Avrom later found out that this individual was an extremely conservative Republican who regarded the Kennedy administration's policies as un-American. Therefore, he was determined to boycott any symbol of the Kennedy image. Somewhat sarcastically, Avrom inquired of the man, "Would you attend an event at the Eisenhower Theater (located in the Kennedy Center)?" "Absolutely not," was his co-workers definitive and inexplicable response.

After considering the matter, Avrom concluded that the official's inflexible attitude was seriously misguided. He surmised that although at times it makes sense to show your rejection of an idea or a concept, however, when the connection is remote, the principle can appear absurd.

Avrom told of a story involving his mother that illustrated the point that becoming so obsessed by rigid advocacy of a strongly held principle can collide with other relevant interests. This incident occurred at a glassware shop in Jerusalem. The owner, an elderly woman, showed his mother some attractive crystal items that were imported from Germany. As his parents had lost many relatives during the Holocaust and as a protest to the horrible atrocities of the German nation, they made it a practice to avoid all German made products. The store owner, when told of this principle, explained that she herself was a Holocaust survivor and that she earned a bare living by selling these German made products.

Avrom's mother appreciated the dilemma she faced. Wanting to support the store owners, she solved her conflict by buying some non-German items in the store. This solution avoided causing financial loss to the owner while enabling Avrom's mother to adhere to her boycott policy.

For instance, you could reflect your opposition to something the Spanish government did by refusing to buy Spanish wine. The action has the potential to hurt the Spanish economy and change behavior if enough people refused to buy Spanish wine. However, if you demonstrate opposition by refusing to eat a Spanish omelet, it will accomplish nothing, and just be plain silly.

The lesson is that rigid adherence to a policy can sometimes cause harmful consequences if one loses sight of the rational basis for a policy. Or as Churchill would say, "good sense."

It is certainly easier to have no conviction. As Groucho Marx quipped, "Those are my principles, and if you don't like them... well, I have others." Rather, embrace your convictions, just make sure you have the good sense not to go too far.

CHAPTER 9 – ONE STRIKE AND YOU ARE OUT!

You CAN NEVER be certain about the ultimate consequences of an event. However, you can be certain about how you decide to react to it. Viktor Frankl, a survivor of Auschwitz, wisely taught, "Between stimulus and response there is a space. In that space is our power to choose our response. In our response lies our growth and our freedom."

Avrom's mother, Sarah, did not learn to drive a car until she was in her late 40s. Although she was well educated and had many talents, driving was clearly not one of them. And as she never felt she had mastered driving; she was always leery and nervous behind the wheel. Sarah never felt secure enough in her ability to drive her children and always asked her husband to drive when he was in the car with her.

One day, Sarah took the family car from the garage and began driving down the alley to main street. A middle-aged woman, Miriam, was walking toward her holding her little baby and the hand of her two-year-old. Although a young woman, she had suffered much as an immigrant who had survived the Holocaust. Her husband, also a survivor, was a sickly man with a serious heart condition, and therefore was only able to find work at a low paying wage. The couple, who had three older children, barely survived on her husband's salary even with the support of the Jewish community.

Sarah, seeing Miriam approach, quickly planned to slow down by stepping on the brake; however, she mistakenly stepped on the gas pedal! Much to her horror, she struck Miriam and the children. Although the children escaped the event with only mild scratches, Miriam suffered severe injuries and needed to be hospitalized for several weeks. Ironically, that period in the hospital turned out to be the first restful interlude she had enjoyed since the war.

As Sarah was clearly at fault, the insurance company quickly settled the claim and paid Miriam a handsome sum of money. With the proceeds, she purchased a laundromat which the family could operate with little training. Fortuitously, the business flourished and, though her husband died shortly after the incident,

Miriam was able to provide funds to send her children to school, college, and one to law school. All of Miriam's children married, had children of their own, and today live happy and productive lives. This all came about because of one false step (on the pedal).

Miriam's story embodied Frankl's message – we are not defined by what happens to us but how we respond to the situation. The key to adopting this mindset is to accept responsibility for your life. Although Miriam had suffered the horrors of the concentration camps, a dying husband in a new land, and a terrible car accident she was never bitter or resentful. She neither accepted victimhood nor placed blame on others. Rather, Miriam chose to move on after each tragedy and strive to make the best of her situation.

Sarah was heartsick that her negligent behavior resulted in such pain to Miriam. She accepted responsibility for the accident, became a caretaker to Miriam's children, and, realizing it was irresponsible for her to drive again, gave up her car keys.

This story highlights the importance of one's attitude to a tragic event; and, that, a horrendous situation may actually be a blessing in disguise.

CHAPTER 10 – A DREAM NEVER TO BE FORGOTTEN

"Intelligence plus character — that is the goal of true education." Dr. Martin Luther King Jr.

AVROM MOVED to Washington, D.C. in 1962 to begin his career as a government lawyer. Living in Boston and NYC, he had witnessed many large demonstrations and parades. So, it was with great interest when, on August 28, 1963, he was privileged to have a firsthand view of the preparations of The March on Washington.

Despite assurances from the organization's leadership that the event would be peaceful, the federal government had been worried radical elements might resort to violence. Proactively, they closed many streets, forbad parking in a large area, cancelled bus routes for the day of the march, and ordered agencies to follow a liberal leave policy. However, not wishing to show actual fear, the government stayed open, even while encouraging workers to take leave and closing all government cafeterias for the day.

Avrom came to work at Pennsylvania Avenue, despite the imposed transportation difficulties and soon realized he was virtually the only person in his office building. He could see the march passing by his office and observed immediately that the marchers were all very well dressed middle-aged peaceful citizens. There were hundreds of police and National Guard soldiers in full view throughout the route to the Lincoln Memorial, where the ceremonies would take place. And, thankfully, there was no sign of trouble from the protesters.

Avrom decided to follow the marchers for the mile walk to the Memorial. When he arrived, he heard a moving performance of "Blowing in the Wind" by Peter, Paul and Mary. This inspirational song would become the anthem of The March on Washington.

After a few speeches by several civil rights leaders, Dr. Martin Luther King was introduced as the keynote speaker. Avrom knew of his background and his political views but had never seen or heard him in person. Dr. King spoke of the significance of the day, the enormous importance of the struggle for greater freedom. The large audience reacted with immense enthusiasm. Dr. King ended his speech with the famous, "I Have a Dream" portion, delivered with such fiery elegance that the crowd responded with wild applause. Avrom recalls his realization at the time that the speech would go down in history as one of the most famous and momentous in American history, equal to the Gettysburg Address by Abraham Lincoln during the Civil War.

The March on Washington was amazingly successful. It brought to light the innumerable injustices of segregation and discrimination that were rampant in many aspects of life in the U.S. It led to the enactment of numerous federal and state laws designed to remove many barriers to social justice and equality. The fact that the march was not violent strengthened the political power of the effort and enhanced the prestige of its leader, Dr. King. He emerged as a national moral leader with broad authority to guide the racial equality effort in a moderate, non-violent manner, achieving much success.

Avrom came away with several observations:

If you have a chance to attend an historic event, do it, as you will learn a great deal from personal observation.

Major political or social movements are greatly enhanced by demonstrations of large, enthusiastic gatherings.

Well-coordinated peaceful assemblage of citizens can be a very effective instrument for change.

A single speech can have enormous influence if it is heartfelt, timely, and delivered with theatrical performance.

Certain events in your life are so powerful that they will never be forgotten.

Lastly, remember, no matter what, as Dr. King taught, "If you can't fly then run, if you can't run then walk, if you can't walk then crawl, but whatever you do you have to keep moving forward."

PART 2:
BECOMING AVROM

CHAPTER 1 – THIS IS THE ONE!

WE HAVE LEarned valuable lessons on finding purpose. This section focuses on Avrom's personal life and gleans wisdom from his fascinating life journey.

In 2005, Steve Jobs delivered the Stanford commencement speech where he famously said, "You can't connect the dots looking forward; you can only connect them looking backwards."

It is only in retrospect that we understand the story of our lives. As life unfolds, it often feels like a series of random happenings bookmarked by a known past and an unknown future. It is for this reason we need the wisdom and perspective of our elders to help us navigate the present.

Two events happened to Avrom when he was 20 that put him on the path to a meaningful, influential, and happy life.

While attending college in New York, Avrom also studied Jewish law at a prominent yeshiva with approximately 300 of the top students in America. It was decided that a yeshiva would open in Los Angeles and Avrom's school was asked to find six volunteers. It was the 50's and the yeshiva was concerned it would be challenging to find even a few students willing to trade a well-established learning environment for a start-up in Los Angeles. To the disappointment of the yeshiva, many of the boys raised their hands to relocate. Avrom chose to stay.

The head rabbi taught the boys a valuable lesson that framed Avrom's worldview. He said no matter where you live, study or work, the place should have *chen* (Hebrew for grace, favor, and charm) in your eyes. Contrary to popular belief, the grass is not always greener on the other side. If we live our lives wishing we could be in someone else's shoes, or in a different place, it can cause unhealthy thoughts and desires and certainly lead to unhappiness.

In retrospect, Avrom's decision to stay was life-altering and led to the next big event in his young life, meeting his future wife, Sarah. Incredibly, Sarah was the only woman he ever courted, and he won her hand without ever taking her on a date.

A friend, together with his fiancé, asked Avrom to drive them to the airport. The friend's fiancé invited her sister and best friend, Sarah, to see her off at the airport (flying was a big deal in the '50s). Avrom picked them up not suspecting what the ride would lead to. Six blocks later he stopped the car at an intersection. The light turned green and Avrom proceeded. However, another car at the intersection sped through a red light and slammed into his car causing it to flip over. Everyone, except Sarah, was able to get out of the car unharmed but Sarah was trapped. Avrom reached behind the seat and pulled her to safety. Unfortunately, she suffered injuries and was hospitalized for over a month. Avrom visited her often and they developed a strong, loving bond. The other patients observed their obvious love for each other and were thrilled when he proposed.

Little did Avrom know that Sarah already knew a year before they met that they would marry. One day in high school she had opened her locker and a yearbook from Avrom's yeshiva had fallen out. The book fell open on Avrom's page. Sarah picked it up and met Avrom for the first time. She intuited then and there she would marry him and even told her mother that night.

Back to Jobs' Stanford commencement speech, "So you have to trust that the dots will somehow connect in your future. You have to trust in something – your gut, destiny, life, karma, whatever."

Avrom met Sarah in a situation that looked disastrous. But he trusted in "something" that told him to pursue her. And so, they married, and together they had an amazingly outsized positive influence on the world. They did this by understanding that what appears bad may turn out to be good and what may seem good may not be so. All you can control is your own perspective. Wherever you are in any given situation – you should work to find the *chen* which is waiting for you to find it.

This powerful lesson has alleviated my concern about the consequences my choices may have when I look back in retrospect. It doesn't matter. You make your impact each day. And once again, back to Jobs, "Because believing that the dots will connect down the road will give you the confidence to follow your heart even when it leads you off the well-worn path; and that will make all the difference."

CHAPTER 2 – THIS IS KINDNESS...

"Be kind whenever possible. It is always possible." Dalai
Lama

Avrom taught me that it takes kindness to do kindness.
It seems obvious, but so hard to truly get right. This
wisdom is etched in my mind and I try to apply it to all
interactions.

Here's how Avrom intuited this lesson almost 80
years ago.

When Avrom was a young child, his mother once
sent him to a delicatessen to buy cream cheese. The store
was busy and Avrom waited his turn. A middle-aged man
pushed his way to the counter. The owner said, "What

do you want?" The man replied, "I am broke and very hungry, could I trouble you for a sandwich?" The owner gestured to him to stand aside and wait. He resumed serving the paying customers, both those who entered before the poor man and those who entered after. The poor man begged again, "The sandwich, sir, please." The owner lost his patience and angrily shouted, "You will get your sandwich, but you have to wait, there are other customers here." Finally, the owner begrudgingly made the sandwich and gave it to the poor man.

Although Avrom was a small boy, the incident had a profound impact on him. He remembers thinking to himself that clearly the poor man was hungry. Why couldn't the owner just give him the sandwich nicely? Why did he have to be so rough with him? All the poor man asked for was two pieces of bread with a little meat. It was such a simple request which would not have taken much from the owner. How much kinder the act would have been if the owner had been gracious to the poor man.

Avrom learned that a lot of kindnesses people do are not done in a kind way. And, unfortunately, you can undo the benefit of a kindness by the way you perform it.

Here's the lesson – it is an amazing thing to do kindness, but we must be mindful that it requires kindness to do kindness. If a friend is sick, it would be helpful to ask them what you can do to assist them, and it would be even more thoughtful to anticipate their needs and just do it. However, we must be extremely aware of how we deliver the kindness. If the recipient senses it was an inconvenience in any way, and we make him or her feel as though it was an imposition, this detracts from the intended kindness.

Doing kindness with kindness sends the message that we care, and that we empathize with the person. Sometimes, the human comfort and connection experienced by the recipient will mean even more than the kindness itself. We need to think through our intention, the consequences, and the delivery for kindness to be felt on the receiving end. Remember it takes kindness to do kindness – etch it in your mind and it will change everything.

CHAPTER 3 – IT COULD BE YOU...

IF WE ONLY knew the impression that our actions or inactions have on others, we would be so much more mindful in life.

As we saw in the prior chapter, the gruff manner that a delicatessen owner exhibited when interacting with a poor man who had asked for a sandwich, taught Avrom that it takes kindness to do kindness.

A couple of years later, on the rough streets of Williamsburg, Avrom's faith was restored when he observed the right way to do kindness. Here's the story.

In 1946, at 11 years old, Avrom left his middle-class home in Pennsylvania to live with his grandmother in Williamsburg (a neighborhood in Brooklyn) for the purpose of advancing in his studies. It was right after WWII and many Jews who had suffered the horrors of the concentration camps in Europe were settling in Williamsburg.

One Friday afternoon, while standing on a corner waiting for a green light to cross the street. Avrom experienced a poignant episode. He saw a man in his 40s approach an older gentleman and say to him softly in Yiddish that he didn't have enough money to feed his family for the Sabbath. Avrom turned his head so as not to embarrass the man. The older gentleman, without hesitation, and without asking any questions, took out several dollars from his pocket and gave it to the poor fellow. He wished him a good Sabbath and left.

The man didn't look like a homeless person – he was dressed in professional clothes and appeared fine. Avrom had never seen anyone who had to beg on the street-corner for food to feed his family. He felt the shame the poor man must have experienced.

Avrom was most impressed by the dignified and kind response of the older gentleman. There was no judgment – he didn't ask whether the fellow was employed or whether he received any public charity. There was no effort to avoid assisting a poor person, nothing but empathy for the poor man's plight.

Although a young boy, Avrom was able to appreciate that no one is immune from needing help. Over the past 60 years, he has been instrumental in raising money and discreetly distributing charitable funds to people in need. Avrom shared with me how surprised I would be at the types of people that come for support – many of those he has helped never expected to be in such a dire situation. He has come to understand that even a well-balanced, successful person can hit a rut.

Here's the lesson – life is precarious, and misfortunes can happen to anyone at any time. It may be a financial need, a family matter, or the terrible disappointment of a perfect dream that didn't materialize. Like the older gentleman on the street-corner, when we see a need, we should immediately help without judgement, generously, and with empathy.

And, as the late Lord Rabbi Jonathan Sacks so powerfully taught, "The good we do does live after us, and it is by far the most important thing that does."

CHAPTER 4 – IT'S ALL ABOUT THAT WALK...

IT IS SAID that if you knew how much your facial expressions reveal to the world, you would wear a mask. This concept equally applies to the impression that is made by the way you walk.

Avrom grew up in McKeesport, located in western Pennsylvania, in the heart of the Rust Belt. Although a small town, it was well known for being the center of United States steel manufacturing.

Avrom and his family lived on the main road leading to the steel plant and were able to observe the differences in the workers. Each day at 8am, and again at 4pm, they anticipated the loud siren blast announcing the changing of shifts. It was in those precious moments that Avrom was taught how to read body language and understand its impact.

Avrom's mother knew many of the workers and guided him in understanding the significance of their body language. She explained that though most of them were assigned the same type of repetitive work, there was a huge difference in their outlook towards their assignments.

"Avrom, you can learn a lot about the world if you just pay attention. Look how some workers walk ploddingly as if their bodies are unwillingly being dragged along. They are hardworking and necessary for the mill, but the job has robbed them of the joys in life. Compare them to the workers who walk with speed, urgency, and high energy. Even though their work is also repetitive, and often boring, they are grateful that it provides them with an honorable livelihood, a home and education for their children." Avrom's mother also pointed out that some found tremendous pleasure and meaning in their work knowing it was helping build the country.

Here's the lesson – we have very little control over our environment, but we have complete control of our reaction to it. As Victor Frankl said, "Our greatest freedom is the freedom to choose our attitude." Our attitude is a personality trait evident in how we walk and how we relate to others. Are we moving with urgency and purpose? Are we adding or depleting energy from our environment? Attitude is an unbelievably powerful quality that truly differentiates us.

Unlike the dangerous and repetitive work found in the 1940s steel mills of western Pennsylvania, many of us are fortunate to have interesting, challenging, and fulfilling jobs. It is beneficial to reflect on how our work serves the important purpose of providing for our families and improving the world in so many ways.

As Roger Miller wisely observed, "Some people walk in the rain, others just get wet."

CHAPTER 5 – REMEDY OF INDIFFERENCE!

WHAT MAKES some people respond to a need while others do not? As Elie Wiesel observed, "The opposite of love is not hate, it's indifference."

The following story illustrates how Avrom saw a need and, without any expertise in the matter, responded and made a difference. To appreciate the story, imagine a world without smartphones, internet, and computers – just the daily newspaper and the 30-minute nightly news.

On September 6, 1970, two international aircrafts (TWA and Swiss Air) carrying hundreds of passengers left Europe traveling to New York City. The aircrafts were hijacked and forced to land in a remote Jordanian airstrip (Dawson's Field). Tensions were high as the Jordanian army surrounded the planes and made contact with the hijackers. They listened to their urgent demand for the release of prisoners held in Germany, Switzerland, England, and Israel. This order included a prisoner captured that day in a foiled hijacking of an EL AL flight. The group threatened to kill the hostages if the prisoners were not released within 72 hours.

Making matters worse for negotiations, a third aircraft (British Air), had been hijacked and taken to Dawson's Field. Finally, after several days with little food and water, hundreds of hostages were released. However, six Jewish men were identified and transferred to a secret location. The hijackers then defiantly blew up three empty aircrafts simultaneously.

Avrom received a call from a fellow Harvard Law School student who had become a prominent and connected DC lawyer. "Avrom, we have to do something! The hijackers are asserting that these six Jewish hostages are U.S. citizens who emigrated to Israel. The U.S. State Department appears to believe them and is, therefore, not taking action."

It was time to act! Avrom and his lawyer friend assembled a group of people to counter the lie that these hostages were Israelis and not Americans. Working around the clock, making phone inquiries to hundreds of hostages and their families, they proved that these Jewish hostages were indeed still American citizens.

At the time, the Nixon administration was very anti-communist. Avrom fortunately discovered that the packaging of the food provided by the hijackers showed that a communist country was backing their cause furthering U.S. conviction. The efforts of Avrom's group convinced high officials in the U.S. government that the hostages were loyal Americans, and that strong action should be taken to get them released.

Over the next couple of weeks, the Jordanian army engaged in heavy fighting with the hijackers. Meanwhile, on September 27th, with the backing of President Nixon, Egyptian President Gamal Nassar, in exchange for certain demands of hijackers, brokered a settlement for the release of the hostages.

Here's the lesson – when you see a need, just act. Indifference is fed by the little voice inside your head that says, "Who am I? What difference can I make to the outcome? Let someone else do it." And, true, the reality is that our efforts will likely not reach the President of the United States, but will reach someone far more important, ourselves. Our job is to simply put in the effort.

Although he rarely spoke of it, Avrom was proud that he had played an important role in the release of the hostages. Content with focusing on the needs at hand without any desire for admiration or recognition has become a recurring theme in Avrom's life. We can all benefit from this wisdom. As President Truman said, "It is amazing what you can accomplish if you do not care who gets the credit."

CHAPTER 6 – KEEP YOUR EYES ON THE ROAD...

WE EACH HAVE a special contribution to make in the world – we need to determine our own unique capabilities, capacities and experiences that differentiate us. When we constantly look at others' lives and try and imitate them and yearn for what they have, we are not living life and benefiting the world.

Avrom has taught me how to embrace and extrapolate the life lessons and wisdom from daily interactions. Each experience, whether positive or negative, gives you something that can improve your life and assist you in making your unique contribution.

The following story is a great example from Avrom on how to reflect on an experience and internalize the lessons.

The year was 1955 when, at 19, Avrom was offered an opportunity to be part of a small group of students who would be assistants at a summer camp in Jerusalem, Israel. Avrom was excited at the prospect and convinced his parents to finance the trip. Other than airfare, the sponsoring organization would pay all expenses, including the cost for an extensive tour of Israel.

Avrom and his four friends began the journey in NYC. After flying from NYC to Scotland, they preceded to London, traveling across the English Channel to Paris, and then through the Alps, and on to Venice. Upon arriving in Venice, they boarded a ship to Haifa. The ship arrived in Israeli waters very early in the morning. When the Israeli coastline became visible, the passengers hurried to the deck. They watched the appearance of the holy land with great anticipation and emotion. Avrom can still recall the overwhelming effect it had on him.

The boys second adventure was about to begin as they went through customs and boarded a train to Jerusalem. They arrived with great anticipation at the school where they would reside for two months.

Life in Israel was very different from the routine these young men were accustomed to in the U.S. They had to get used to a different language, different kinds of food and, most significantly, different attitudes about life and social style.

One especially intriguing difference concerned the influence of politics on so many facets of Israeli daily life. Newspapers were allied with specific political parties. Many banks and health institutes were operated by political organizations and some schools were run by political entities. More notably, the population was consumed by politics and spoke about political issues constantly. During the summer of 1955, elections were held in Israel, heightening the preoccupation of the citizenry with politics. Avrom found the level of political concern to be somewhat shocking and amusing. The large number of political groups, some with extreme agendas, seemed quite strange to someone from a country with only two major political parties.

One day toward evening, Avrom was on a bus heading back to the section of town where his school was located. The school was on the edge of town and the last stop of the bus route. As the bus proceeded on its route, almost all the passengers got off, leaving only a handful of patrons. Two men got into a forceful debate about the forthcoming elections and began shouting at each other with strong language and extreme anger. Suddenly, the driver – a man in his late 50's – pulled off the road, stopped the bus, left his seat, and joined the heated political argument.

Fortunately, Avrom was not on a tight schedule that day and did not suffer from the delay caused by this strange diversion. He mused about what would happen if such an incident occurred in the U.S. He realized that such a skirmish was very unlikely as Americans in 1955 were not as obsessed with politics.

Avrom was an undergraduate student at the time, majoring in Political Science. He wondered which was the better system – extreme involvement in national politics or relative indifference. Regardless of the right answer, Avrom came away with the realization that foreign travel is an important ingredient in learning how different cultures function. It is also something that all young adults should be encouraged to experience if circumstances make it possible.

Most importantly, Avrom learned, regardless of how passionate you are about politics, if you are a bus driver, you should focus your attention on the traffic!

CHAPTER 7 – I WILL NOT EVEN LOOK!

IMAGINE A world where we weren't so quick to dismiss others because they don't think and believe like we do.

Avrom's grandfather was born in Hungary. He came to the U.S. just prior to WWI and became a well-respected professional Hebrew schoolteacher in McKeesport, Pennsylvania. He was well versed in traditional Jewish studies and was Avrom's first teacher. Avrom loved learning from his grandfather even though he could be quite stubborn.

Avrom went away for school but would visit his parents and grandparents often. He enjoyed sitting outside in his grandfather's yard on long summer evenings. In 1958, on one of these visits, Avrom mentioned to his grandfather that the first U.S. orbiting satellite, the Vanguard 1, would be visible above Western Pennsylvania later in the evening.

Avrom's grandfather responded, "God created the universe with a sun, moon, planets and stars. There is no such thing as a satellite." Avrom began to argue the point, but to no avail. "Grandfather, just look at the sky at 8:12pm and you will see for yourself." He stubbornly retorted in Yiddish, "Ich vel afilu nisht kiken," loosely translated as "I will not even look."

As a young man, Avrom learned several things from this incident.

Smart people do not always hold smart views.

You can respect and learn from people on a selective basis. Don't accept pronouncements that don't seem correct; be your own final judge.

Even educated people believe in some myths.

New realities may pose difficulties to strongly held religious beliefs. Rather than deny the veracity of the obvious facts, figure out how different truths can be reconciled.

In the end, both religion and satellites have survived, and they have lived happily ever after.

You can be a great expert in one field while being totally ignorant on another subject.

You can be so terrified of the unknown that you dare not investigate its existence.

The greatness of Avrom was how he extrapolated a small interaction with his grandfather into the foundational life lessons listed above. He looked up to his grandfather. And, while a lesser person might have lost respect and faith in him, Avrom chose not to.

He returned to his parent's house and at 8:12pm, looked at the sky and saw the Vanguard. He didn't tell his grandfather. Of course, he wouldn't have believed it anyway.

CHAPTER 8 – I NEVER FORGET A TOWN!

Avrom's mother came to the U.S. as a teenager from Hungary. Her family lived in McKeesport, Pennsylvania, a small steel-mill town where her father was the chief rabbi. Once, a prominent rabbi from Lithuania, Rabbi Kahaneman (also known as the Ponevezher Rav) spent a weekend at her home, where he was a guest rabbi at her father's synagogue.

Many years later, after WWII, the Ponevezher Rav became a world-famous religious leader and founder of a large yeshiva in Israel. He would occasionally travel to Miami to meet with wealthy supporters. Avrom's parents happened to be in Miami on one such visit and Avrom's mother asked a rabbi-friend to introduce her to the Ponevezher Rav.

"It is a great honor to the meet the Rabbi again. It brings back memories of my excitement as a young lady when the Rabbi honored our small community with his presence; it was a moment I will never forget." The Ponevezher Rav replied, "It is an honor to meet you, but you are mistaken, as I was never in McKeesport." Avrom's mother didn't relent, "But, you were there. You have been to hundreds of communities and it is understandable that you forget visiting our small, ordinary town. But I did not forget your visit – it was so meaningful to me that I cannot possibly be wrong about it happening." The rabbi responded, "Madam, you are correct that I have visited many hundreds of communities around the world. And, I am proud to say, that I have never forgotten any of those communities. I assure you I was never in McKeesport."

Most people would have let it go but not Avrom's mother. She was a strong, independent woman with a first-rate mind. "Not only were you there for a weekend and our honored guest, but I recall the sermon you delivered as its message was so profound, I can still repeat it." She proceeded to relate back to him the 2000-year-old Talmudic teaching and the novel interpretation he shared in his sermon those many years ago in McKeesport. When she finished, the Ponevezher Rav excitedly said, "That's mine! That's my thought!"

Avrom learned several important lessons from this event:

Even great minds can make a mistake.

Really great people admit an error.

There are sometimes truths that you hear, or incidents that you experience, that make such a profound impression on you that you never forget them.

Many mistakes that we make stem from an error in a premise which we mistakenly think is absolutely true. Like, I don't recall his name, but I know it starts with an "M". If that premise is wrong, you'll never figure out the real name because it doesn't, in fact, start with an "M".

If you are certain about a fact, don't let anyone (even a venerated leader) convince you otherwise.

Many years later, a friend of Avrom told him that the Ponevezher Rav was so moved by the incident that he told the story to an Israeli journalist. Imagine the conviction required to stand your ground and to do it confidently and respectfully – never easy, especially when the other person is an influential and revered leader.

CHAPTER 9 – BROADWAY MEETS STATUE OF LIBERTY!

"You never know when a moment and a few sincere words can have an impact on a life." Zig Ziglar

MOST PEOPLE can't recall the names of all their teachers, or specific items they learned, even from teachers that they do remember.

Avrom has been teaching regular Talmud and Bible classes to adults for more than 60 years. When he was in the 6th grade (in 1947), an English teacher, Mr. Kirschenbaum, made a lasting impression with the technique he used to teach a technical point of grammar.

He came into class, went to the blackboard, and wrote, "I saw the Statue of Liberty walking down Broadway." He asked the class, "What's wrong with that sentence?" The class shouted, "The Statue of Liberty can't walk." The teacher responded, "Okay, now, you fix the sentence without adding or subtracting a single word."

The class was filled with very bright students. Many attempts were made, but no one succeeded in fixing the sentence under his rules.

Mr. Kirschenbaum strode back to the board, "Now watch this: Walking down Broadway, I saw the Statue of Liberty."

Some in the class shouted, "You said no additions or subtractions." The teacher responded, "I said no words can be added or deleted. I didn't say anything about punctuation." He explained what a complex sentence meant and when it should be employed. He taught nothing else that day.

By creating controversy and excitement, and with a little dramatic flair, Mr. Kirschenbaum got his message through. In addition to comma usage, Avrom learned an important teaching technique from Mr. Kirschenbaum, not forgotten in almost 75 years.

Of course, not all teachers can use this technique (we're not all good at theatrics) and not all subjects provide the opportunity. But generally, in education and in any field where persuasion is important, we are impressed by external factors, which the presenter should employ. This technique is used in the media. Effective politicians have this skill in their quiver. Advertisements employ drama all the time.

Here's the lesson – presentation matters. Spend as much time designing the delivery to your audience as you do creating the content. We need to make the first encounter attractive to create curiosity and a lasting effect. Just as a priceless work of art in a cheap frame lessens the art, our ideas will not be fully appreciated or lasting if we skimp on the packaging.

CHAPTER 10 – LOOKING ISN'T SEEING...

"Never underestimate the big importance of small things."
Matt Haig, The Midnight Library

WE HAVE DISCUSSED in several chapters how Avrom's childhood experiences in McKeesport, Pennsylvania, a small steel-mill town, profoundly shaped his life. Avrom has a remarkable ability to internalize seemingly simple events into life changing lessons. The following story occurred when he was nine and he still remembers it as if it were yesterday.

Avrom's parents had a housekeeper, Anny. She was a pleasant and simple woman who was good at her work.

On a very hot summer day, Avrom's parents were in search of some relief from the oppressive heat. They decided to have dinner at a park just outside the town where it was much cooler. They asked Anny to join the picnic. During the meal, she whispered to Avrom, "I am 56 and this is the first time in my life that I have ever been outside of McKeesport."

Avrom was shocked. Anny had never even been to Pittsburg (12 miles away) which had museums, theater, professional sports, tall office buildings, and universities. All her social contacts were limited to the people in town who were mainly employed in the local steel mills. It made Avrom sad for her and appreciative that in his young life, he had already seen more of the world than she.

Avrom gained a new appreciation for travel and determined that he would never let what happened to Anny happen to him or his family. In fact, Avrom intentionally visited, in addition to most of the United States, many foreign countries. For the numerous years that his in-laws lived in Israel, he and his wife visited there annually. Each time Avrom tried to travel there by a new route, through a different foreign country. He and his wife learned to appreciate the many differences in the ways people live, work, and think.

However, while traveling and interacting with people from different cultures is certainly important and opens up our eyes to many things, it can fool us into thinking we are more open than we may be. It takes tremendous strength to open oneself to new ideas and perspectives.

As David Henry Thoreau said, "It's not what you look at that matters, it's what you see." A good start to really seeing is constantly asking yourself, "Am I Anny?"

PART 3:
UNLEASHING SEYKHEL (STREET SMARTS)

CHAPTER 1 – NO LONGER IN BROOKLYN!

Avrom understood at a young age what a fulfilling career should be and acted on it with complete clarity. Equally clear to Avrom was his uncompromising integrity, kindness, and moral fortitude.

It is one thing to be honest and kind in government sinecures or by adopting a pollyannaish view of human nature. However, Avrom directly engaged in an often rough and deceptive world. He did not let it impact who he was but rather strived to mark every interaction with his honesty, kindness, and a smile.

The following story brilliantly illustrates how Avrom employed tact and smarts to protect his integrity and teach all those around him in the process.

At the end of Avrom's career he was a senior lawyer at the U.S. Department of Energy presiding over a significant number of oil company lawsuits. A certain big oil company was represented by one of the most prominent and famous lawyers in America (we will call him Mr. X) who was well regarded and revered by many including the government lawyers and politicians. Mr. X was in his 80s at the time and came to D.C. to meet with Avrom, U.S. Department of Energy leadership, and government lawyers to discuss two lawsuits involving his client. Mr. X told Avrom that he would agree to let the Government drop one lawsuit if the Government dropped the other. The politicians and government lawyers bizarrely were so enamored by Mr. X they pressured Avrom to accept the peculiar settlement.

Avrom smiled at Mr. X and said, "When I was growing up in Brooklyn, the big kids played a game with the little kids where the big kids said to the little kids, 'I bet you a quarter that if you give me a nickel, I will give you a dime.' The little kids couldn't believe their luck and handed over the nickel and the big kids delivered the dime. Afterwards, the big kids said to the little kids, 'now, give me a quarter, you lost the bet!'…. Mr. X, we are no longer kids in Brooklyn." Avrom didn't accept the offer.

Avrom spent weeks and weeks trying to figure out Mr. X's angle (a complex web of interrelated dealings) and when he did, he traveled four hours to NYC to meet with Mr. X. Avrom said to him, "I figured out what you are up to. I am going to tell you what it is, but you are going to deny it. I just want you to know that I know the game you are playing." After Avrom explained, Mr. X vehemently denied such a ludicrous explanation but Avrom politely said again, "I just want you to know that I know." The meeting ended.

The message here is though we cannot control the actions of others, we must be able to identify whether we are being spun (as Reagan said, "Trust, but verify"). And if we are being spun, we need the wisdom to appreciate that there are times to keep it to ourselves, times to use wit to subtly let the other person know, and times to end the relationship.

The big kid, little kid story is etched in my mind. It reminds me to think critically. And, hopefully, now will remind you to, as well. Moreover, I may have once or twice even said, "When I was growing up in Virginia, the big kids played a game with the little kids…" Most importantly, what I learned from Avrom is the critical importance of retelling ourselves about the games big kids play with little kids, so that we can protect the little kid in each of us.

CHAPTER 2 – CHECKMATE!

Avrom has taught us how to find fulfillment, how to use judgment to advance in an organization, and how to navigate in an honest and kind way. And now Avrom will teach us the most important yet the most elusive and enviable quality of *seykhel*, which in Yiddish loosely translates as street-smarts.

A more modern definition of *seykhel* can be found in season seven of Game of Thrones where Littlefinger advised Sansa, "Don't fight in the North or the South. Fight every battle everywhere, always, in your mind. Everyone is your enemy, everyone is your friend. Every possible series of events is happening all at once. Live that way and nothing will surprise you. Everything that happens will be something that you've seen before."

Avrom was a civil servant in various agencies throughout his career. Every four years, the politicians and political appointees would change and regardless of the party in charge, Avrom never took sides. Avrom employed *seykhel* to navigate the ever-changing agendas, tense political hearings, and inevitable scandals. The following are a couple of stories that illustrate this.

All about who you know.

The Senate held a hearing to determine whether the U.S. Department of Energy settlement with a mid-sized energy company involved corruption. It turned out that owner of the company's son (Mr. M) was the deputy director of another agency. Thousands of cases were settled each year and Avrom, a senior enforcement official, was not aware of this case nor did he know Mr. M. A certain senator was antagonistic to Avrom and Avrom quickly discerned that the senator suspected him of settling the case on extremely favorable terms and was determined to prove it. During a break, Avrom waited outside of the men's room and when Mr. M exited, Avrom introduced himself. Later in the hearing, the senator asked Avrom if he knew Mr. M and Avrom said he did. The senator excitedly thought he connected the dots of abuse. The senator followed up and said, "when exactly did you meet Mr. M?" Avrom responded, "Ten minutes ago in the bathroom." The room erupted in laughter. Avrom's boss was up next in the hearing and Avrom advised him to introduce himself to Mr. M when he came out of the bathroom, which he did. Avrom knew the senator would ask his boss the same question and when he did the room again erupted in laughter. Avrom cleverly showed the senator there was no corruption.

Stuck in a hard place.

As a senior career lawyer, the most difficult part of Avrom's job was maneuvering through the politics of the current administration and the opposing party. In one instance, the administration recommended cutting Avrom's budget by 90%. The Chairman of the House Budget Committee (let's call him Chairman Y) was from the other party. The administration did not want Avrom testifying at the hearing and instead had his politically appointed boss testify. The boss knew nothing. Each time Chairman Y asked the boss a question, he turned around and asked Avrom. Avrom purposefully sat far enough behind the boss so that everyone in the room could tell that he was calling the shots. Impatiently, Chairman Y asked Avrom to come up front. After futilely resisting, Avrom unwillingly moved to the testifying table.

Chairman Y asked Avrom how large a staff it would take to handle the present caseload. Of course, Avrom knew it was not possible with the proposed reduced staff to handle 1700 cases. However, if he said that publicly, he would be fired. Avrom responded that the President is the one who submits the budget, and Avrom's job was to answer questions, not to propose an alternative budget.

Chairman Y said, "I know that. I didn't ask you to propose a budget. I just asked how many people it would take to perform the enforcement task." Avrom replied, "Perhaps, I wasn't clear, and I apologize. It is not my function to submit the budget; the President does that." Angrily, Chairman Y said, "I'm giving you one more chance to answer my question. How much staff would it take to handle the present number of enforcement cases?"

The hearing room, packed with oil company lawyers, lobbyists, and government officials, became very hushed and tense. Avrom realized he was in a terrible pickle. He decided to say nothing, he just glared at the Chairman for several moments in total silence.

Finally, Chairman Y said, "Let me tell you a story, Mr. Avrom, about President Calvin Coolidge. He had a portrait commissioned, as did all previous presidents, to hang in the White House. Coolidge kept the portrait in a closet in the dining room. The president invited a friend for dinner and showed him the portrait. Coolidge said to his friend, 'What do you think?' And like you Avrom, he didn't respond at all. Coolidge said, 'I think so too.'"

Avrom knew he was being set up, so as Chairman Y told the story, he focused on every word trying to find a funny way out. Chairman Y asked Avrom if he thought the story was relevant. Avrom knew just how to respond,

"Yes, Chairman Y, the story is very relevant because I too don't want to hang in the White House."

Chairman Y cried with laughter, and after realizing he was outplayed, he moved on. Avrom was being set up by both sides and escaped unharmed.

Seykhel or street-smarts is the ability to grasp what is really going on, to weigh the possibilities of outcomes like a chess player, and decisively act with cleverness. Clearly, not everyone can be a Chess Grandmaster, but we can all learn how the game is played. And the first rule is to understand the inner driver and desires of the players, including yourself. Next, you need to consider all possible moves and appreciate that your best action might be to stay neutral until a later time (e.g., Avrom's jokes to get out of an impossible situation). Lastly, we must accept that the other side is rational, and paradoxically, in the process of grappling with the other person's opposing views or motivations; we begin to understand the other side and partially absorb it.

CHAPTER 3 – IS LAUGHTER REALLY THE BEST MEDICINE?

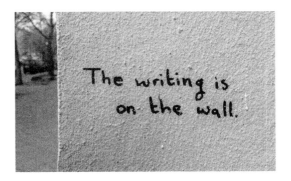

"DON'T count your chickens before they hatch." "If you want something done right, do it yourself." "The early bird catches the worm."

All languages are rich with common idioms and sayings that have survived the test of time and have a certain degree of authoritativeness. An aha moment in my life was when I learned that how we express and package our thoughts is as important as what we actually say.

A brilliant thought leader I know told me that he only started really connecting with his executive clients when he added the phrase, "the research shows" before sharing his unique insights. The wisdom didn't have the same punch until the clients thought it was backed by research. Similarly, in a Seinfeld episode, Jerry and Elaine were discussing the smarts of fortune cookies at Chinese restaurants and Jerry quipped "No one's reading any rolled-up messages in a knish."

On January 1, 1968, President Lyndon Johnson signed an executive order prohibiting any "direct or indirect transfer of capital to or within any foreign country or to any national outside of the United States." The prohibition was directed to U.S. citizens who own 10% or more of a foreign business. The order authorized the Secretary of Commerce to implement the provisions and establish the Office of Foreign Direct Investments (OFDI). He formed OFDI as a response to the growing deficit in the U.S. balance of payments – more money was leaving the U.S. than coming in. The OFDI called the most prestigious law firms and banks and ordered that they send over their brightest and most ambitious employees to work in the agency. With very little oversight and under the cover of an emergency order, the agency of approximately 100 individuals quickly promulgated numerous regulations. Avrom was recruited to join as head of enforcement.

One day, Avrom walked into the office and was greeted by an anxious crew of these young muckety-mucks. They asked him to join them in the conference room and explained their dilemma. "Avrom, we are so glad you are here; we may have gone a bit too far on issuing one of the regulations. Might it be possible to liberalize it?" Avrom understood early on that shtick is not limited to Hollywood shows; it is just as important to "perform" in the business world. Avrom put his left hand in his upper left shirt pocket and his right index finger on his lips and pensively swayed his head. The muckety-mucks couldn't take the suspense, and one of them shouted out, "Avrom, tell us what the Talmud says we should do." Avrom thought for a few minutes, raised his right index finger and said, "The mouth that prohibits is the mouth that permits." You could hear a pin drop as they contemplated this profound teaching, looked at each other and at the same moment, and elatedly shouted, "We can do it!"

Avrom recognized that we all have blind spots – things that are obvious, but that we cannot see. Clearly, the young regulators should have had the common sense to realize that if they wrote the rules, they could change the rules. But, again citing the Talmud, "A prisoner cannot release himself from the prison he is in." And here is the lesson – rules are a lot like common sayings, we tend to accept them. "It is because it is." The regulators assumed they were bound by the rules simply because they were the rules. And if the folks who write the rules or make the decisions believe they are immutable, how much more so does the average person. We do ourselves a disservice if we don't challenge assumptions, prior decisions and longstanding practices. Often, an obvious solution or better course of action is present if we only take the time to identify, breakdown, and challenge the status quo.

CHAPTER 4 – SHADES OF GRAY...

THRILLER MOVIES are full of suspense, plot twists, and characters trying to outsmart each other. There are similar dynamics in the business world, in the context of corporate takeovers and board maneuvering. Unfortunately, there are also petty politics, turf wars, and destructive undermining.

Avrom certainly saw his share of the good, the bad, and the ugly as the only thing certain in Washington is the periodic, pendulous shift in the political leadership. In 1981, the Reagan administration took over and Avrom had a new set of politically appointed bosses. As is common with all new presidencies, the transition team prepared briefs on key government career employees.

Although confidential, Avrom saw his briefing which described him as intelligent, but gullible, and unaware of the doings of his department, including the numerous leaks. It also stated factually that he was from New York and had attended Harvard law school.

The transition team assumed that because Avrom was from New York, which he wasn't, and had graduated from Harvard, that he must be a Jewish liberal and could not be trusted. As is often the case with assumptions, this one created an alternate reality which, while influencing and impacting the behavior of others, did not comport with the truth. Most noticeably, it skewed the way Mr. B, a feckless politically appointed leader, viewed and treated Avrom.

Mr. B was small-minded and habitually impeded Avrom's work. In one instance, he blocked information that was required to be shared with a particular Congressional oversight committee. Instead of waging an unwinnable battle, Avrom decided the best way to get the information to Congress was to change the narrative.

Avrom drafted a confidential memo and addressed it to six individuals, including Mr. B. He personally delivered this highly confidential memo to each person and put a check next to the recipient's name to document that it had been received. However, Avrom intentionally did not give Mr. B his copy. Instead, he asked one of his trusted staff members, "How might this document reach Congress?" The staffer understood what Avrom meant.

The Congressional committee received the memo and assumed it had come from Mr. B. Again, the assumption was it must be from him as it was the copy with a check next to his name. Avrom knew Mr. B rarely read his memos so he couldn't say that he never received it because perhaps he did, and he would have to admit to the committee that he didn't always read his memos.

How could Avrom deceive anyone? He is the epitome of conscientiousness and honesty; it seems so out of character. Let's revisit the story. What did we miss, which is an important question we should always ask.

Congress was entitled to the information withheld by Mr. B and Avrom got it to them with the least amount of damage possible. From the standpoint of the committee, Mr. B provided the information through the proper chain of command as he was required. However, from his perspective, though he suspected that Avrom had leaked the memo to Congress, he was not positive how they got it. In the end, as long as the committee didn't realize anything was out of the ordinary, Mr. B was relieved that he had dodged a bullet.

Avrom had 'killed two birds with one stone'. He did his job and got the information to Congress without undermining Mr. B. And, more importantly, he also subtly winked to Mr. B that he was no fool, and, if necessary, could outmaneuver him. Only Avrom and Mr. B were aware of this mini thriller, which is exactly what Avrom intended. As a result, Mr. B respected Avrom and allowed him to do his job.

Here's the lesson – not everything is black and white. Sometimes what may seem like the wrong thing to do in one circumstance becomes the right thing to do in another; and, sometimes what's right and wrong is not clear. You must choose between options that are gray and think through all possibilities. And, as a plaque on President Obama's desk reminded him daily, "Hard things are hard."

CHAPTER 5 – PULL IT TOGETHER!

IN A LATER chapter, Avrom will teach us that ideas unfold in their own time. We need the space and time to understand the challenge, sit with it, analyze it, and trust that we will have a flash of insight. But what happens when the insight doesn't come, and a solution appears impossible?

Here is an incredible story from Avrom and actionable insights you will want to add to your toolkit.

In 1973, due to American support of Israel in its war with Egypt and Syria, Arab oil producers cut off oil exports to the U.S. This caused oil prices to soar from $3 to nearly $12 a barrel and shed light on America's dependency on Middle Eastern oil.

Numerous attempted legislative solutions were enacted. For instance, legislation capped the price at which U.S. oil companies (referred to as "Big Oil") could sell "old" oil – that is, oil discovered from domestic wells before a certain year. However, "new" domestic oil could sell at market rates. This was intended to depress prices without disincentivizing new domestic drilling operations. Not surprisingly, Big Oil preferred to sell new oil at the higher market rate and pulled much of the old oil from the market. The U.S. Department of Energy (DOE) fought many times with Big Oil on the matter of what oil was truly "new".

Moreover, legislation exempted from price controls wells that produced 10 barrels a day or less, known as "stripper wells". Litigation ensued as the DOE and Big Oil battled over the classification of several thousand oil wells from 1973-1981, seeking to deny stripper well status. Appreciating this would be protracted and contentious for years to come, a federal judge in Kansas (we will call him Judge T) granted stripper well status to the wells in questions allowing Big Oil to charge market rates. Judge T was overruled and as the litigation continued the rules got even more complex (the difference between the capped rate and market rate was required to be placed in escrow, which by 1986 had ballooned to $1.4 billion and involved 40,000 claimants).

Additionally, special privileges were given to subsidize independent and small U.S. refineries. A Robin Hood type program was implemented requiring "advantaged" refineries to pay "disadvantaged" refineries, which also created its share of litigation.

In 1981, President Reagan terminated pricing and allocation controls. Over the next few years complex, multi-party litigation ensued. Big Oil was fighting Big Oil and together fighting the 50 states, which were fighting among themselves; meanwhile, the Federal government was fighting on all fronts. Collectively, approximately $4 billion (equivalent to $10 billion today) was embroiled in this intractable web of litigation.

At this time, Avrom was a senior lawyer in the DOE. He was on the front-line of all the litigation and understood how deeply the parties despised each other. He also realized that each of the lawsuits individually had little chance of being resolved. But Avrom had a hunch; if he could consolidate all the cases and look at certain factors holistically, he might be able to get the various parties to agree to a settlement.

Avrom knew that Judge T was vacationing in Miami and more than anything wanted to clear these cases from his docket so he could relax at the beach. Avrom flew down to Miami, met Judge T for coffee, and explained his plan. The Judge was ecstatic and believed they had a chance. He said to Avrom, "You work on Big Oil and the States and I will handle Congress." "Deal!" Judge T then let out a sigh of relief and said to Avrom, "Bless you, my son!"

Over the next eight months Judge T and Avrom traveled the country, managed big egos and delicate compromises. Eventually, the plan gained traction and coalesced in an omnibus settlement. The monumental settlement, which was the largest civil settlement at the time, was approved in July of 1986 by Judge T in Kansas.

As a mentor of mine used to say, "If you're wrestling an alligator, it's better to be on top." No one at the DOE told Avrom to fight this alligator but he saw an interesting problem, the resolution of which would both be professionally fulfilling and help provide much needed funds earmarked for the citizenry of the states that were parties to the litigation. If he did nothing, the litigation would go on for years. Avrom wrestled the alligator and came out on top, but, other than Judge T and a handful of lawyers, Avrom never told anyone else about the instrumental role he played, until now.

Here's the lesson – sometimes the solution to a multi-faceted problem is not linear and must be approached holistically. A solution to each sub-issue may be impossible, but a holistic solution may solve global issues and mitigate the impact or the relevance of smaller ones. Counterintuitively, the holistic solution may be palatable to all even though the individual solutions would be palatable to none.

When you a hit brick wall, think broadly, bravely, and boldly. Consider how multiple problems, even seemingly unrelated ones, can be added to the mix!

CHAPTER 6 – MAKE THE CALL...

THERE ARE certain moments in our lives when opportunities present themselves. Yet, many times we either don't notice them, underestimate their significance, or simply fail to act.

In 1984, Avrom was a senior lawyer in the U.S. Department of Energy (DOE) and leading an investigation against U.S. oil companies (referred to as "Big Oil"). He received a phone call from the Assistant U.S. Attorney for the Southern District of New York who knew about Avrom from his work on an unrelated Iran oil prohibition. "There is a man, Mr. F, a crude-oil reseller, who got out of jail yesterday. I believe he has information that will be useful to you and I strongly suggest you contact him." "What information might that be?" asked Avrom. The man replied, "It is grand jury confidential information; take my word on this and talk to him."

Avrom received hundreds of leads which mostly led nowhere. But he had a hunch about Mr. F and the next day, without telling anyone, he flew to Texas to see him. They met in a rural town in a nondescript trailer for what turned out to be a memorable opportunity for Avrom. Mr. F was an angry, rugged man of action, who had had an axe to grind against Big Oil ever since they had failed to help him with his legal troubles.

Mr. F explained in detail the illegal activity of certain Big Oil companies, crude-oil resellers and law firms. Avrom was in shock! He had spent years in vain investigating what was known as the disappearing old oil problem and now the answer was so clear.

Fortuitously, on the plane back, Avrom sat next to the in-house counsel of a well-known Big Oil company. He casually asked about the crude-oil reseller arrangement and was told by the lawyer that he had learned one of their traders was involved in this illegal activity. The company had immediately rebuked this trader and returned all the profits. Avrom was relieved to have confirmed the illegal activity and that at least one of the Big Oil companies was playing by the rules.

In the prior chapter, we explored Avrom's role in the 1986 monumental Big Oil settlement ($10 billion in today's money) – the settlement involved shenanigans stemming from the 1973 oil embargo that caused oil prices to rise from $3 to nearly $12 a barrel. This separate investigation took place a few years earlier and involved Congressionally imposed price controls on "old" oil (oil that had already been produced from the ground but not yet refined before a certain year). There was a substantial amount of old oil and the DOE was empowered to police Big Oil to ensure price controls were followed. Nevertheless, after a few years, it became obvious that the total amount of old oil produced was not showing up in the old oil being refined. A significant amount of old oil, strangely, "disappeared" somewhere in the system causing consumers to pay more for gasoline and heating oil. This was a matter of great concern for the DOE and a riddle Avrom had spent years trying to solve.

The DOE had teams of auditors housed permanently in Big Oil offices to investigate the disappearing old oil. In fact, a CEO of a Big Oil company once approached Avrom, "My folks tell me that you have 175 auditors in my company; this is outrageous!" Avrom acted surprised and told him he would immediately investigate the matter. He didn't want to further upset the CEO by telling him in fact that they had 350 auditors!

In that first and last meeting with him, Mr. F explained to Avrom what the auditors were unable to uncover: the secret behind the disappearing old oil. Big Oil had deals with crude-oil resellers and through a system of exchanges engineered by the crude-oil resellers had kept a system of records that were not true. In short, they illegally had two sets of books where they exchanged certificates of old oil for certificates of exempt oil; this is how they made the old oil disappear. Mr. F knew which Big Oil and which oil were involved and he also knew the names and sizes of the transactions (totaling hundreds of millions of dollars). This was all the information Avrom needed to proceed against Big Oil. Avrom, in retrospect, was abundantly thankful he had followed his intuition and seized on the opportunity to meet with Mr. F.

In 1981, President Reagan had terminated pricing and allocation controls. Those cases remaining a few years later in 1984 involved clean-up of enforcement work. Naturally, the Reagan administration, although wanting to move on, had no choice but to continue with the cases which were in process. They were not happy when Avrom wanted to start new investigations based on Mr. F's findings. He knew he needed to tread lightly and employ his well-honed seykhel (street-smarts).

Avrom called each of the crude-oil resellers involved in the illegal activity telling them, "I want to talk to you and I suggest you bring your lawyers – I know the information you provided the DOE is false and you have another set of books. You can either cooperate with me and be absolved of wrongdoing or we will launch a major investigation that will bankrupt you and likely put you in jail." All of the companies agreed to the deal. Avrom wisely turned these deals into cases against Big Oil.

The DOE settled with Big Oil for hundreds of millions of dollars. This all happened because Avrom took advantage of an opportunity when it presented itself. He had an intuition that his meeting with Mr. F would be a major event and he should not walk away from it.

Here's the lesson – each moment is pregnant with potential; it may be a small kindness that only you can do or a meeting that unlocks the secret of disappearing old oil! If you are curious and contemplate why the opportunity is presenting itself, listen to your intuition, and seize the moment, magic can happen.

CHAPTER 7 – WHAT'S IN IT FOR ME?

"Tragedy is when I cut my finger. Comedy is when you fall into an open sewer and die." Mel Brooks

IN BUSINESS, we must juggle many balls at one time, navigate shifting priorities, and execute on current and desired initiatives. The secret to why so few are successful at this is simpler than you may believe.

In the early 70's, during the Nixon administration, Avrom received a call from a politically appointed senior leader of the Department of Commerce (we will call him Mr. C).

"Avrom, could you tell me something about them Hasodem?" Avrom replied, "Well, the first thing I will tell you is that they are not Hasodem, they are Hasidim." Mr. C stood corrected. "See I knew I called the right guy; you know everything Avrom. I have this problem; Congress just passed a law subsidizing loans to minority businesses. Some of them Hasidim, as you say, applied as members of a minority. I need you to tell me about them so I can decide whether they constitute one."

Avrom explained to Mr. C that the Hasidim, a subgroup of Orthodox Jews, have a very particular modest way of dressing, live in insular, self-sufficient communities, and mostly speak Yiddish. Mr. C seemed perplexed by this and Avrom realized his definition would not suffice. He instinctively pivoted the conversation in a different direction.

"Mr. C, you mentioned you have children. I suspect there are times when you come home from a long day at work and see them sprawled out on the living room floor watching an inappropriate television show. When you ask them indignantly 'Who said you could watch this?' do they reply, 'Who said we have to ask anybody what we can watch?'" Mr. C laughed, "Yes, I know that feeling – happens all the time." "Well, that doesn't happen to the Hasidim because they don't have televisions in their homes." Mr. C was shocked and, on the spot, declared the Hasidim a minority, and eligible for the program.

Avrom came away with two realizations. Firstly, none of the substantive points he made about the minority status of Hasidim had any currency with Mr. C, a highly intelligent and sophisticated person. Using the relatable story of the television made the needed impression. And, secondly, unfortunately, the reality is that important decisions often are based on trivial matters.

Here's the lesson – no matter how smart you are, how fancy your slide deck, elegant your Excel model, or obvious your business strategy, unless you make the information personal and meaningful, the desired objective will be difficult to achieve. When we are immersed in an objective it is easy to think action will "just happen" but it doesn't – it requires effective communication. We have many powerful tools at our disposal. But we must remember that they are just tools and do not replace the important qualities of relevance and relatability.

CHAPTER 8 – MAGIC 8 BALL!

THE LATE CEO of Intel, Andy Grove, used to say about decisions, "[They] don't wait…. You have to make them when you have to make them." It is hard enough to make decisions individually, but anyone who has worked in a large organization appreciates the difficulty when many people are involved.

During the latter part of Avrom's career in government, he was a senior lawyer in the U.S. Department of Energy. Very often decisions were required that involved uncertain outcomes.

Each new proposed regulation had ramifications that were far-reaching, and many specialists were needed to evaluate factors that had to be considered. The litigators had a weighty decision to make as to whether or not big oil companies would vigorously oppose the regulation. And, if big oil challenged the regulation in court, which court would likely be chosen and what would be the chance of prevailing. The politicos would predict the congressional reaction, political ramifications, and media response, while the economist had strong views based on a myriad of assumptions.

Each group played their own game of 'chess' with possible outcomes and were hell-bent on their positions. They were stymied because of internal division and differences of opinion on what was the best course of action.

Avrom understood that when the normal course of analysis doesn't yield a definitive result, people are eager to run to a non-analytical source. It could be a miracle worker, clairvoyant, or some other irrational omen such as a Magic 8 Ball, anyone or anything that can provide direction and decisiveness.

Avrom's modus operandi was to stay neutral, avoid playing any political games, and wait until the individuals involved came to him to resolve the uncertainty.

"Avrom, you are a wise man of God, what should we do?" He knew they wanted a direct answer, and not a technical analysis. He wisely chose to employ his well-honed theatrical skills. He would pretend there was a crystal ball, hold his hands with his palms facing it, close his eyes and look pensive for a few moments. "The oracle can only say what he sees." He would then authoritatively tell them, without explaining his reasoning, what he thought should be done.

Avrom enjoyed watching the joy that appeared on their faces. He had relieved them of the anxiety of making a decision that was chancy. Avrom learned from Rabbi Moses Isserles, a 16th century halakhist, "There is no joy greater than the resolution of doubt."

Here's the lesson – unlike Avrom, few of us are in the position to make far reaching decisions; nevertheless, our sphere of influence is larger than we think. We should appreciate that often reasonable and smart people can have opposing views and that they are seeking anything upon which to grab. Ultimately, a decision must be made.

Avrom's crystal ball shtick likely will not work for us. But, digging deeper, it wasn't just the crystal ball that gave Avrom power, it was his unusual ability to accept full responsibility for his decisions. Regardless of where we are in an organization, we are empowered, even though perhaps unwillingly, to make difficult decisions. As David Ogilvy said, "There is no shortage of people with brains — however, the spinal column seems to be in much shorter supply!" Leadership is the acceptance of responsibility.

CHAPTER 9 - WHAT'S THE PLAY?

Don't assume that your opponent is stupid or that he has your best interests at heart. Everyone has an angle – you must know your opponent's strategy and revise your own accordingly.

Many years ago, Avrom was called for jury duty and during the jury selection process the judge asked him to come to the bench. He proceeded to ask Avrom if he knew the defendant's attorney, Mr. Smith. Avrom vaguely recalled he had dealt with Mr. Smith in the past on a personal insurance matter. Though Avrom assured the judge that he could render a fair and impartial verdict, Mr. Smith exercised a preemptory challenge to have Avrom dismissed from the case.

On his way back to his car, Avrom recalled the incident with Mr. Smith years prior. His wife, Sarah, had been in a serious car accident in which a woman in another car was injured. The woman sued for $200,000 in damages. Sarah's insurance company, represented by Mr. Smith, was not able to settle, and the case went to litigation. After interviewing Sarah, Mr. Smith asked that Avrom call him.

Avrom phoned Mr. Smith as requested. Strangely, Mr. Smith said that he hadn't asked to be called. Avrom quickly realized that Mr. Smith was up to something and there was significance as to who initiated the contact. Avrom wasn't yet sure of the angle. "Mr. Smith, assuming I was the one who initiated this call, what reason might I have to wish to speak to you?" Mr. Smith replied, "The claim against your wife is for $200,000, but you only have $100,000 in liability insurance. I will fight the case as best I can but, but if we lose, you will be personally liable for any amount over $100,000. It would be advisable for you to engage the services of your own lawyer."

Though couched as concern from Avrom's personal liability, Avrom suspected that Mr. Smith was really trying to protect himself and the insurance company. Avrom responded, "I am sure you'll do your best, but you have already failed to settle the case. If you lose, you may be liable for malpractice and your insurance company will have to cover your expenses. I'm sure you have insurance in an amount greater than I do. If I have my own lawyer, I won't be able to sustain a case against you. So, can you explain how I will be better off with my own attorney?" There was a loud silence from Mr. Smith and the call quickly ended.

A few weeks later, Avrom received another call from Mr. Smith. "Avrom, we discussed your wife's case internally, and the insurance company would like to settle for $100,000. What is your opinion on this settlement strategy?" Avrom asked Mr. Smith why his opinion mattered. Mr. Smith explained that if the $100,000 offer was rejected, and the case was lost in court, Avrom could claim that it was negligence to have offered such a large settlement at the outset. On that basis, Avrom could sue for malpractice. Avrom replied that he had not thought of that possibility and thanked Mr. Smith for suggesting it. Avrom then said, "Based on that suggestion, I have no comment at all." Ultimately, the case did settle for $100,000, Avrom bore no liability, but Mr. Smith did not forget the episode and did not want Avrom on his jury.

Here's the lesson – life moves fast, and it is much easier to go with the flow and assume that people have your best interest at heart. It is hard work to figure out what angle someone might have and certainly not healthy to be guided by constant mistrust. However, when there are clues that trigger doubt, we shouldn't dismiss them out of hand. Recognize that others may be wiser than they appear and may not be acting with your best interest at heart. We need to do the slow thinking of figuring out the subtleties and competing interests and have the wherewithal to punch back.

CHAPTER 10 – CAN DO CANDOR!

"You can't buy a good reputation; you must earn it." Harvey Mackay

Avrom has a stellar reputation which he earned with impeccable integrity, honesty, and kindness. In 1985, Avrom was immersed in a controversy on possible misdeeds involving Mr. W, the Deputy Director of Office of Management and Budget. Mr. W allegedly asked the Department of Energy (DOE) to speed up a pricing case against his father's oil company. Senator Eagleton was convinced Mr. W, with the assistance of the DOE, fixed the case.

Avrom, as a senior DOE lawyer who led a large group of lawyers, accountants, and auditors investigating oil companies, was a crucial witness in determining whether the DOE illegally helped Mr. W. The Wall Street Journal (WSJ) reported on the hearing and explained that Avrom was not a political appointee but rather a Harvard Law School graduate who had been a civil servant for 23 years. Further, the WSJ remarked, "You would have had to work hard to dream up such rotten luck for the prosecution – the man is an ordained rabbi."

Avrom testified there was no political pressure, no wrongdoing, and the case was settled in a routine matter. Senator Eagleton bluntly declared, "I don't think he is telling the truth," and proceeded to cross examine him. The WSJ explained how Avrom controlled the exchange, "Senator Eagleton baited the witness in the grand tradition, but the witness parried the thrusts and baited the senator right back."

Because Senator Eagleton did not produce a shred of evidence, other senators came to Avrom's defense. Senator Rudman stated, "Let me make a comment for the record…I have understood the testimony as much as anyone in this room, and I understand candor when I hear it. I want to say for the record that any kind of allegation that you [Avrom] have not told the truth here is based on no facts whatsoever; it is simply based on someone wanting to prove a point they want to prove, and I am a little offended as a member of this panel that anyone wanted to make this charge against you." The hearing ended with Senator Eagleton not producing any evidence of wrongdoing from Avrom or the witnesses who followed him.

Benjamin Franklin noted, "It takes many good deeds to build a good reputation, and only one bad one to lose it." Avrom was determined not to let Senator Eagleton interfere with his apolitical work as a government attorney. He respectfully stood up to him, defended his good name and demonstrated the importance of candor.

PART 4:
INSPIRING LEADERSHIP

CHAPTER 1 – CHARACTER IS POWER

POWER IS A curious phenomenon. Although it manifests itself in almost all interactions, we tend to have an uncomfortable relationship with it. Unfortunately, we rarely get it right.

Avrom started his government career at the Federal Trade Commission (FTC). After making a great first impression he was anointed as the 'chosen one'. A few years later, the leadership recommended him for a prestigious and desirable position with the Senate Antitrust Committee. They were looking for a hotshot young lawyer and Avrom was the ideal candidate.

At the beginning of his interview with Mr. S, the Senate Committee Chief of Staff, Avrom exchanged pleasantries. Mr. S then looked at Avrom's resume and said, "Oh, wait a minute, we have a problem. I never hire anyone from Harvard Law School." Avrom politely inquired, "May I ask why?" Mr. S impatiently responded, "Harvard Law graduates are all too arrogant." Avrom smiled, "That's okay, I happen not to be one of them." "Sorry, Avrom, that is my principle; this interview is over."

It is a well-known but often not followed axiom to be careful how you treat people. What you do to others has a funny way of coming back to you.

Fast forward 22 years to find Avrom in charge of choreographing a massive civil settlement (equivalent to $10 billion today) with big oil companies. Ironically, Mr. S was the lawyer for the gasoline retailers, one of the many parties involved in the omnibus agreement. Mr. S had much at stake personally with this transaction as the settlement would be significant. He nervously remembered his first encounter with Avrom and apprehensively said to him "I know who you are; I certainly hope you don't hold that incident against me." At that moment, Avrom remembered the interview. There was total silence in the room. Avrom paused and pensively tapped his right index finger on his lips, and with a veneer of seriousness said, "Mr. S, I am a religious person. I am going to pray to God that I have the strength to overcome the incident." Everyone, except Mr. S, erupted in laughter.

There is a power dynamic in all relationships. Mr. S was in a precarious situation – his client would not hesitate to remove him as their lawyer if he threatened their financial settlement.

Avrom did not hold the incident against Mr. S and was not planning to mention it to anyone. However, appreciating that power is a valuable tool to get things accomplished, Avrom had framed his response for the necessary effect. As Alice Walker said, "The most common way people give up their power is by thinking they don't have any."

Here's the lesson – we should not ignore the role of power in relationships. As a leader, and we are all leaders in one way or another, if we pretend we don't have power, we are being dishonest and will be ineffective in leading. Even worse, if we abuse our power, and are cruel or selfish with others, our leadership likely will be harmfully ineffective and even damaging.

The role of the leader is to build trust and security with others so that while we have power, we will not abuse it. And, as we have learned from Avrom in earlier chapters, the more we develop our character and treat others with respect and kindness, the wiser and more effective we become. "Character is power." Booker T. Washington

CHAPTER 2 – HOW DO YOU MAKE IT?

"Men occasionally stumble over the truth, but most of them pick themselves up and hurry off as if nothing had happened." Winston Churchill

AVROM TOLD me lots of stories about his life and his friends and a common theme that emerged from these successful individuals both professionally and personally is they each exhibited good judgement. And perhaps the greatest indicator of judgment is humor. Early in his career Avrom worked in the Federal Trade Commission. One morning he was called into the office of a senior official and asked for his advice on a tricky situation. The government had a settlement where a large company was required to divest of one of its manufacturing plants. Unfortunately, on the day of the divestment, a fire destroyed the plant.

The senior official asked Avrom what the government should do. Avrom said it was a complicated and novel area of law and as he wasn't involved in the settlement he would need time to study the matter. The senior official kept pushing Avrom for an immediate answer and was frustrated by Avrom's hesitation.

Avrom looked at the senior official, smiled and told him the following story:

Saul and Morty, two old friends from NY, surprisingly bump into each other at a Miami hotel. Saul says to Morty, "What are you doing here? You haven't taken a vacation in 50 years from your belt factory in NY!" Morty says, "The strangest thing happened, a fire destroyed the belt factory and while we are negotiating with the insurance company my wife suggested we take a vacation." Morty asks Saul, "What are you doing here? You also haven't taken a vacation in 50 years from your coat factory in NY!" Saul says, "Like you, the strangest thing happened, a hurricane flooded the coat factory and while we are negotiating with the insurance company my wife suggested we take a vacation." Morty says to Saul, "I am so sorry to hear about your loss, but I have to ask you a question – how do you make a hurricane?"

The senior official burst into laughter. He then phoned the manufacturing plant executives and recounted the joke. Immediately, the CEO of the company called the Commissioner screaming how offended he was that the government would suggest his company would burn down its own manufacturing plant. The Commissioner protested that he would never suggest such a thing but countered that he was in favor of a full investigation.

Later that same day, the Commissioner summoned Avrom into his office. He nervously entered and the Commissioner looked at him and said, "Avrom, I have a question for you – young man, how do you make a hurricane?" The Commissioner patted Avrom on the back and laughed.

It is said that nothing reveals more about a person's real character then their laughter. Avrom knew exactly why, when, and how to use humor. The hurricane joke got him out of a difficult situation and signaled to the Commissioner he was someone with great judgment. And here is the important lesson – leaders expect rising stars to have technical knowhow, integrity, and drive. The real differentiator is judgment. It imbues trust, confidence, and limitless potential. Avrom used humor to demonstrate his impeccable judgment, but each person must determine what special character trait exemplifies his or her judgment. Like a hurricane, once you get it right it will clear your path to success. And that is how you make it!

CHAPTER 3 – 13 CENTS...

WE HAVE SEEN how Avrom brought a sense of laughter and playfulness to navigate delicate and important situations. Certain events, like a Senate hearing, are clearly important and heighten our need to be attentive to the moment.

Avrom told me about an old book called, *May This House Be Safe from Tigers*, written by Alexander King, a comedian, raconteur and eccentric personality from the 1950's. King tells a story about a friend who whenever he would leave a house visit, would clasp his hands and say, "May this house be safe from tigers." On one such visit, a person said to him, "What good does saying that do?" The friend responded, "Seen any tigers lately?"

Avrom taught me that life is less complicated than it appears – we just need clarity of what is important and not to be distracted by futility. This is hard because we are often blinded by the seemingly important tigers of the moment. When we look back on life, we remember we were in a rush to do something but can't remember what.

The following story sheds light on the effort required to have such clarity.

As a young boy, Avrom's father had a newspaper distribution business and Avrom helped in the office. Each afternoon, Avrom would spend hours with his aunt on the bookkeeping. He recalls that once after finishing their work they had 13 cents more than they should have based on the number of newspapers sold. The aunt said we need to redo all our work. Avrom confusingly asked his aunt, "What is the big deal, we are only over by 13 cents?" His aunt taught him a valuable lesson. She said, "The net number doesn't tell you anything, other than there is an error – it is a net number, we need to figure out all the movements."

On a professional level, I have used the story many times to bring home the point that we must examine the various components of the numbers. When we catch ourselves dismissing de-minimis amounts, we should ask ourselves is 13 cents really only 13 cents? This story reminds me to do the necessary slow thinking and analysis required. On a personal level, this story is much deeper. It has taught me that each event or interaction in our life stands on its own. You can't net them. Oft times, we rationalize that we can make up important events or replace one interaction with another. Each moment has unlimited potential and possibilities. Every positive interaction, word, and deed matters, and impacts those around us and the broader world far beyond what we can understand.

CHAPTER 4 — WAIT FOR IT...

A GREAT PErson once said that all beginnings are difficult. A beginning is half of everything while the other half of everything is executing the right timing. As King Solomon/Byrds wisely realized, "To everything there is a season and a time to every purpose under heaven."

There is a certain beat to life that it seems only a few people really get. Avrom mastered the perfect timing of a joke to get out of sticky situation, "How do you make a hurricane?", the perfect timing of a story to signal you are no fool, "We are no longer kids in Brooklyn", and the perfect timing of kindness to become an avuncular figure in so many lives.

In an earlier chapter, we met Mr. X, a revered and legendary American lawyer, who proposed to the U.S. Department of Energy an absurd offer to drop one of his client's lawsuits if the government dropped the other. The ultimate decision was above Avrom's pay grade and thus he could have let it go. However, it deeply bothered him that someone so smart would make an offer so seemingly dumb. It was a challenge that took Avrom weeks to process and when he did, he visited Mr. X to let him know he solved the mystery.

As for the business world, Avrom taught me how essential it is to get the timing of an idea correct. Every bold ambition is encountered with obstacles and barriers. These exist because of bureaucracy, embedded processes and inertia to change. We need grit, gumption, and guts to overcome. But, first, we need to master the art of perfectly timing when an idea has been fully crystalized, and it is ready to be implemented.

We need to take people on the journey of our ideas, but only by executing perfect timing will we be successful. We must recognize that although we feel compelled to tell someone, and are bursting with enthusiasm, if the idea is not ready, we do tremendous damage. An analogy would be in the simple egg; you need the pressure of the boiling water and the exact amount of time for it to cook properly. If you take the egg out too early, you may ruin it. Ideas also need time to brew sufficiently. As Einstein said, "it's not that I'm so smart, it's just that I stay with problems longer."

Ideas unfold in their own time.

The litmus test to know when an idea is ready is when you can explain it with absolute clarity and simplicity. It is very easy to explain a correct idea and very complicated to explain a wrong idea. Again, back to Einstein, "If you can't explain it simply, you don't understand it well enough."

Then there is the timing of when to present. All mankind marches to the beat of a universal rhythm – the seasons, sunrises, and sunsets. Companies also beat with their own ebbs and flows. It's easy to miss this cadence as we get lost in the regimented schedule of the quarter close, deadlines, and scheduled meetings. We need the self-awareness and mindfulness to balance these competing demands and be tuned in when the company is ready for the developed idea.

We may wonder if others will question why it took so long to figure out something so ostensibly simple. We must remind ourselves that educated people will understand that the simplicity and clarity is the result of deep analysis and nurture. And when everything aligns – the idea has fermented and is bursting to come out and the world is ready for it – magic happens. Timing is everything!

CHAPTER 5 – NO SURFING ALLOWED...

THERE ARE volumes of books and courses on effective public speaking. But perhaps the most important skill in this type of communication is understanding the difference between content creation and content delivery.

In college, Avrom took the standard required public speaking course. The class assignment was for each student to present a biographical speech which the rest of the class would critique. The professor would deliver comments, focusing on what was well done and what needed work. Avrom selected President Harry Truman as his topic and deeply researched his life and contributions. As fate would have it, Avrom was chosen to go first.

Here is how Avrom started the speech: "I'd like to talk to you about a man, he was a U.S. Senator, [pause], he was Vice President of the U.S., [pause], and then he was President of the U.S., [pause], his name is President Harry Truman." No one before Truman had held all three positions. Avrom designed the introduction to engage his classmates in the process of determining who the subject of his biography could possibly be.

As the students left the classroom, the professor asked Avrom to stay behind. "Great job in grabbing the attention of the students! I am giving you an A for the speech and an A for the course; your preparation was exemplary as was the important lesson you taught the class."

Avrom demonstrated to his classmates how one should operate in two modes when preparing and delivering a speech. Regarding preparation, it is essential to invest sufficient time and become a master on the subject matter, unearthing and making sense of many facets and subtleties beyond what could be gleaned based on a cursory assessment. Next, time and effort in the delivery should be comparable to the development of the presentation itself. It is important to be skilled in explaining the topic in a concise and simple manner, omitting points which are not critical to your message. It is the art of curation.

These two modes can be compared to an iceberg – while you can only see the tip of the iceberg, you know that there is tremendous expanse below it. Counterintuitively, in order to effectively deliver at the level of the tip, you must understand the topic at the full depth of the iceberg.

Avrom intensely studied Truman and yet figured out a clever way to grab his classmate's attention with very basic information. Because Avrom's introductory, three-line, summary was rooted in a profound understanding, the students sensed the depth beyond the information presented and were drawn to the presentation. As W.B. Yeats said, "Think like a wise man but communicate in the language of the people."

CHAPTER 6 – IT NEVER ENDS...

"The price of greatness is responsibility." Winston Churchill

A MENTOR liked to say the key to success in the corporate world is to be "agile, mobile, and hostile." She believed that constant movement within and between companies quickly adds valuable tools to your toolbelt. But, what does it say about responsibility?

In 1968, President Lyndon Johnson, as a response to the growing deficit in the U.S. balance of payments, formed the Office of Foreign Direct Investments (OFDI). In short, OFDI prohibited U.S. citizens from sending cash to foreign owned businesses unless they had received a special authorization. Avrom was asked to join this prestigious agency. OFDI was shut down after six years and the rules were obsoleted allowing U.S. citizens to invest in foreign owned businesses.

Many years later, Avrom, while working for the Department of Energy, received a call from a wealthy businessman (let's call him Mr. B) who owned a wheelchair manufacturing company in Indiana. Mr. B was a 50% owner of a UK based joint venture. Due to the OFDI regulations at the time, Mr. B was unable to fund his share of the business and was sued in an English Chancery court by his UK partner for failing to provide his cash contribution.

The dispositive question was whether Mr. B could have obtained a special authorization to have sent the funds. He knew Avrom was one of the few individuals who understood the defunct regulations. Mr. B asked Avrom if he would testify concerning whether he could have received an exemption.

"Avrom, this could cost me many millions of dollars, please help me; I will pay you whatever you want." Avrom assured Mr. B he would help but added, "I will testify on two conditions – the hearing will be on an American holiday, so I won't miss work and I refuse to take any compensation; I am doing this as a favor for a fellow American."

At the hearing, the judge was extremely gracious and impressed with Avrom. He appreciated his obvious expertise and thoughtful preparation as he explained why Mr. B could not have received an exemption. As Avrom left the courtroom, Mr. B thanked him and handed him $1,000. Avrom refused, "The understanding was there would be no fee." Mr. B replied, "I feel badly for taking you away from an American holiday and just don't feel right, please take the money and buy your wife something." Avrom shook his hand and told him, "I will not take the money and if I want to buy my wife something, I will pay for it myself. I wish you continued success."

Failing to grasp the significance of responsibility, Mr. B didn't understand why Avrom would not take the money. Avrom had drafted these regulations and felt, even a decade later, responsible for their consequences. As Mahatma Gandhi taught, "It is wrong and immoral to seek to escape the consequences of one's acts."

Here's the lesson – regardless of whether we are "agile, hostile, and mobile", we must appreciate that we are accountable and responsible for our actions. This applies even many years later and even if it is an unintended consequence. When you truly internalize this message, you will find your decisions today will be infused with more care and attention because the responsibility never ends.

CHAPTER 7 – KNOWING WHEN TO POKE...

"Don't poke the bear" is a popular expression in the corporate world; it is much safer not to challenge the status quo. The skill is knowing when and how to implement this strategy.

The 1970's oil crisis was causing havoc to the U.S. economy. It was time for the government to rethink and retool its energy policy. In 1977, by merging several government organizations, President Jimmy Carter created the U.S. Department of Energy (DOE). The goals of this newly formed organization were to promote energy conservation and develop alternative sources.

Avrom was honored that he had been chosen as the division director of a large bureau in the newly formed DOE. He reported directly to Mr. G, a politically appointed head of a bureau and a former brigadier general. Mr. G was an imposing leader under whom Avrom correctly ascertained it would be difficult to serve.

"Avrom, the Secretary of Energy has allocated grants worth millions of dollars to each of the bureaus in the agency. However, to receive this money, the approval of a bureau-wide committee is needed. I want you to represent our unit on the committee." Avrom sensed Mr. G had ulterior motives and the thought was reinforced when, as Avrom left the room, Mr. G winked and said, "Oh, Avrom, by the way, I know you are a smart guy, but for this assignment I need you not to be so smart."

Each month Avrom met with the committee and quickly learned the game – classic Washington quid pro quo – keep your mouth shut and approve each other's requests. The philosophy was that unanimity would give all participants cover.

The Committee was told, "The country is suffering from an energy shortage that is increasingly becoming an emergency. We need to make some difficult decisions immediately. Our proposal is to study whether Americans would prefer reducing heat in the winter or reducing air conditioning in the summer."

Avrom thought this study was a good idea and, as he was interested in pursuing it, inquired "How much do you need?" The requestor responded, "We propose giving a certain professor in Minnesota $150,000 so he can spend the next 12 months studying how to do the study." Avrom laughed, "I thought my job was to make the jokes." "We are not joking." Avrom incredulously responded, "This is absurd, you are telling me he needs a year to put together a plan on how to do the study without actually doing the study. By the time he finishes making a plan, it may be too late to positively affect the energy crisis. I would like to be a team player and cooperate, but I can't agree!"

When Mr. G became aware of Avrom's response, he angrily rebuked him, "What the heck, I told you not to be so smart! Just agree with the committee." "Sorry, Mr. G, I can't sign off to such governmental waste! But, if you give me until tomorrow morning, I will design the study plan myself; and, I will need 12 hours not 12 months!"

Avrom's suspicion was confirmed. Mr. G's plan had been to distance himself from the committee's decisions so as to avoid any career repercussions. To accomplish this, he was willing to make Avrom his lackey.

Here's the lesson – we need to appreciate the powerful forces that hold us back from the uncomfortable and the risky. For most people, one's job is necessary for their livelihood and sense of purpose. It is much easier to play along than to 'poke the bear'. And as the Yiddish saying goes, "If you want people to think you are wise, agree with them."

A well revered CEO of a large corporation explained that, if you feel strongly enough in your gut about an issue, you must act. Ask yourself how important the results would be and if the timing is right to affect the change. If the answer is yes to both, respectfully 'poke the bear'.

CHAPTER 8 – WHISKEY AND HERRING!

WHAT MAKES a leader? Everyone you ask will tell you something different. Avrom was fortunate to learn what makes a leader in his 20's and it changed all his interactions going forward.

He arrived in the Washington D.C. area with an unusual combination – he had rabbinic ordination from one of the most respected and revered rabbis in the world, a Harvard law degree, and fluency in Yiddish. His combination of success in both the religious and secular worlds gave Avrom the credibility at an early age to be entrusted to start a new synagogue and serve as its first president and acting rabbi.

The synagogue's congregation included young professionals starting their careers and families and older businessmen, many of whom were Holocaust survivors and primarily spoke Yiddish. Meeting the needs of all these congregants could at times be challenging.

After Saturday morning services, the synagogue had a kiddush (small reception with desert and coffee). People would socialize and Avrom would teach a class.

A few weeks after Avrom started the kiddush, a group of elders came to him and said in Yiddish, "Der eulm vil shnaps," which loosely means the people who really run the world want whiskey. Avrom responded, "No, we will not have whiskey, it will disturb the quality of the class." The next Saturday there were two bottles of whiskey on the kiddush table.

Again, a few weeks later, the group of elders visited Avrom and said in Yiddish, "Der eulm vil hering." The elders wanted herring to accompany their whiskey. Avrom said, "No, we will not have herring, it will make a mess." The next Saturday morning there were two bottles of herring on the kiddush table.

Then a few week later the gentleman came back and said in Yiddish, "Der eulm veln nit hering in jar, der eulm vil frish hering." The people no longer wanted herring in a jar, they wanted fresh herring. Avrom told them, "No, we can't afford fresh herring – it is too expensive." The next Saturday morning there was fresh herring on the kiddush table.

Avrom was confused, as he was the president and acting rabbi of the synagogue, he took it in his head that he was in charge. Why weren't the people listening to him?

After much contemplation, he realized the challenge of leadership and how easy it is to fool oneself that he should make all the decisions due to his position and smarts without considering the opinion of others.

Here's the lesson – a good leader does not ride roughshod over the wishes of others but instead is sensitive to, and acknowledges, their wants and desires. Of course, this must be balanced by the times where one must have the courage to make decisions on one's own due to competing demands or a broader perspective.

Great leaders, like Avrom, lead with their human greatness. It is the extraordinary ability to make each person feel that they count, that they are of supreme importance and have limitless potential. When people feel valued and heard, they trust and accept the leader's decision. Try viewing each person this way, and your life will be much more enjoyable, rich, and surprising.

CHAPTER 9 – CANCEL THE ORDER!

"It is not enough to give orders they must be obeyed."
Napoleon Bonaparte

WHEN WE ARE not heard, or listened to, the reason is likely a character flaw in ourselves rather than others.

In earlier chapters, we learned Avrom was a senior lawyer in the U.S. Department of Energy (DOE) who led numerous investigations against U.S. oil companies. Many of these investigations, including price controls, were due to policies enacted in response to the 1970's oil crisis. Specific legislation exempted "stripper wells" – wells that produced 10 barrels a day or less-from price controls. The difference in the price of controlled oil and stripper wells was significant.

A case arose regarding a Native American tribe that had significant oil production on their reservation. The calculation of how much oil they produced indicated they were slightly over the 10 barrel a day requirement (in fact, they were at 10.8 barrels). The tribe was investigated for years and was fined a few million dollars plus an administrative citation.

The tribe complained to their congressman stating what they perceived to be unfair treatment. In turn, the congressman put a lot of heat on the DOE. Of course, this heat filtered down from the Secretary of the DOE to Avrom's bureau. Avrom reported directly to the head of the bureau, Mr. G.

As a former brigadier general, Mr. G was accustomed to his staff listening to him and acting on his orders. He called a meeting of his staff and told them the problem, "Go down to the reservation and find me one more damn oil well!" [As the tribe was only slightly over the 10-barrel limited, a single well would decrease the average below 10 barrels.]

The staff understood that Mr. G wanted them to lie about the existence of another well. Mr. G did not command the respect of his team. In fact, they detested him. The collective response of the staff was, "No way, we will not do it, the law is the law and applies to everyone equally."

Mr. G believed his staff would fold when subjected to his stern, confrontational and bullying leadership. He was wrong.

Mr. G had stubbornly demanded that subordinates engage in unethical behavior and cut off any discussion. Imagine if Mr. G had rather said, "I have a problem, I can't handle the pressure, any ideas on how we can solve it?" This vulnerability, humility and attempt at collaboration may have yielded a creative and legal way to get below the 10-barrel limit, which was everyone's objective.

Here's the lesson – instead of giving orders, ask questions. "Might it be possible?" "Do you think this will work?" "What is wrong with my analysis?"

Questions show others you respect and value them. It also stimulates creativity. And, most importantly, it creates accountability. "What do you think – should we cancel the order?

CHAPTER 10 – DON'T BELIEVE IT...

IN A PRIOR chapter, we learned that, on January 1, 1968, President Lyndon Johnson, issued an Emergency Order prohibiting all transfers of capital funds to overseas subsidiaries or divisions of U.S. persons, except as may be authorized by regulations issued by the Secretary of Commerce. The Emergency Order was a trade imbalance (more money was leaving the U.S. then coming in) which was resulting in an emergency for U.S. security. In fact, the imbalance was caused by the huge cost of the Vietnam war, a fact that because it was politically damaging was left unstated.

The Office of Foreign Direct Investment (OFDI) was swiftly created in the Department of Commerce.

Many normal civil service rules were by-passed: Funds for operation were taken from a certain Treasury source; Congressional appropriations were avoided; and certain conflict of interest rules were ignored.

The government asked certain large corporations and law firms to send some top employees to temporarily join the OFDI, and Avrom was asked as well. Several major N.Y. law firms sent top senior associates to draft the complex regulations needed to implement this fledgling and novel program.

Chase Manhattan Bank transferred a senior executive named Chuck to serve as Director of OFDI for a one-year term. Chuck was smart, well-liked, and well-respected for his business acumen and his esteemed reputation. He dressed in expensive suits befitting a Wall Street leader.

One day at a meeting, one of the Jewish N.Y. lawyers said, "Chuck, did you know that Avrom just bought a suit with two pairs of pants for $19.99 at a department store sale?" Chuck, reflecting on what he spent for his clothes, was amazed and asked where he could get such a bargain. "You are not eligible, it's only for Jews!" Surprisingly, Chuck accepted that claim and went on with the meeting.

The incident showed how many very talented people can be duped by false claims. Chuck should have known that in Washington D.C., it would be unthinkable to limit sales to Jews. It would be bad policy and bad business. No one ever heard of such a thing. Yet, Chuck just assumed the fact was true because someone he trusted told him so.

Here's the lesson – we need to check out the veracity of asserted facts when we sense some doubt. Propaganda can be very effective because the public is gullible, and leaders know the public can be fooled.

PART 5:
BEING A MENSCH

CHAPTER 1 — AVUNCULAR

THE SECRET to being a great leader or employee is simply to behave as the leader you wish to follow or the employee you love to manage. Daily practice of this will stretch and transform you. Being an exceptional leader or employee is worthwhile, but it is certainly much more rewarding to be recognized as a wise, avuncular figure with deep kindness and an insightful mind.

In an earlier chapter, we learned that after graduating from Harvard law school, Avrom started his professional career at the Federal Trade Commission (FTC). He was assigned to Mr. S to mentor him through the organization. Mr. S was an intransigent sourpuss and considered Avrom a young whippersnapper. It bothered Mr. S greatly that Avrom was his equal in the organization.

Mr. S tried to ignore Avrom but eventually he was ordered to work with him. When they finally met, Mr. S dismissively said to Avrom, "I have no time for you, take these 30 cases, read them and come back if you have any questions." Avrom studied the cases. They all involved price discrimination where companies were illegally charging competing buyers different prices for the same items or services. The practice of the FTC was to issue cease and desist letters and litigate the matters. Once the Court ruled, the company had to stop the activity. Avrom quickly figured out the game companies were playing – it was cheaper to hire lawyers to protract the litigation for as long as possible.

Avrom wrote a memo to Mr. S suggesting a clever and simple fix to the problem by applying retroactive penalties to stop the companies from delaying the litigation. Mr. S read the memo and said, "Listen kid, I don't know who you think you are, but I am going to only say this once, rip up the memo and tell nobody about it. We are done here kid, get out." Avrom moved on. A few weeks later, unrelated to Avrom's memo, the Chairman of the FTC issued the same order Avrom had suggested in his memo. At 12:30am that night, Mr. S's boss called Avrom screaming and cursing at him for insubordination. Of course, not realizing that Avrom had no connection with the Chairman and that it was purely a case of (almost) simultaneous invention, he concluded that Avrom had gone to the Chairman.

Avrom initially denied having anything to do with it but Mr. S's boss refused to believe him. Avrom then had his aha moment and realized it would be best to let Mr. S and his boss think he had the ear of the Chairman. From that moment on, Avrom had tremendous power.

As Avrom progressed through life, he grew to become someone whose wisdom and counsel became widely sought-after. He had outsized influence across the government far beyond his position. In his personal life, thousands of people continue to request Avrom's advice on personal, professional, and communal matters even though he holds no official role in the community.

How did he do it? It is not what you know, it is what people think you know. Taken cynically, this implies that puffery is the way to make it. At its heart, however, this idiom is more about self-confidence and assurance, which goes hand in hand with humility. Counterintuitively we must strive not to be the person in the spotlight, rather the person who sits when everyone else stands and comfortably and quietly directs from the corner. This flies in the face of everything our culture tells us about personal branding, self-promotion, and bravado. It is the desire and confidence in who we are to let others shine and make them significant. As Viktor Frankl said, "If you treat people to a vision of themselves, if you apparently overrate them, you make them become what they are capable of becoming."

What a simple yet powerful idea – the way we want to be treated has more to do with the way we treat others than it does about manufacturing how others should treat us whether through position, intimidation or demands. We all have the potential to become an avuncular figure dispensing our unique brand of insights and wisdom. Start practicing now.

CHAPTER 2 – LONGER ROUTE MAY BE PREFERABLE...

It takes kindness to do kindness. Identifying another's need when others don't and anticipating another's feelings is, in and of itself, an act of kindness. Kindness is just like any other muscle. The more we work it, the better we get at using it.

Avrom's childhood experiences in McKeesport, Pennsylvania, a small steel-mill town, profoundly shaped his life. In the 1930's and 40's, McKeesport had, out of a population of 55,000, a few thousand Jewish residents. Only a handful of these Jewish residents were fully Sabbath observant Orthodox families. As observant

Jews, they didn't drive or work on the Sabbath as it is a day of rest, celebration, and physical and spiritual rejuvenation.

Many of McKeesport's Jews owned retail establishments and closing their businesses on Saturday would entail substantial financial sacrifice. To add to the dilemma, the steel mills paid their employees on Fridays and Saturdays making the Sabbath an important shopping day. This led to many Jews in the area having to make the difficult decision to not observe the Sabbath fully.

The synagogue where Avrom's family worshipped was about half a mile from his home. On Sabbath mornings, Avrom enjoyed the interesting conversations he and his father would have while walking to the synagogue. Once Avrom asked his father why they always took the long way home. This route took much longer and was especially difficult in the cold winter months. Avrom's father explained that the shorter route would take them past a store owned by a Jewish man who was deeply embarrassed by his perceived need to open his business and desecrate the sacred Sabbath.

Avrom was a small boy at the time but never forgot the lessons he learned from the above interaction. These meaningful lessons have shaped the past 80 years of his life.

It is unkind to cause someone else to feel embarrassed.

This is true even if that person's shame is caused by his own misdeeds.

Often, you can avoid causing embarrassment with a very minor sacrifice on your own part (such as taking the longer way home).

True kindness entails thinking very carefully about the remote possible harm your actions may cause (it was entirely possible that the store owner would not notice Avrom and his father walking).

Avrom benefited from his father's deep moral, ethical, and religious convictions and behaviors. However, it is never too late for any of us to start exercising our kindness muscle. The more we do so, the more sensitive we become to noticing potential opportunities for kindness.

CHAPTER 3 – LASTING IMPRESSIONS...

THE IMPORTANCE of making a good first impression is widely accepted. Yet it surprises me how few people internalize the importance of this truism and actualize it. Woody Allen famously quipped, "Eighty percent of success is showing up." Showing up is certainly important but it will not differentiate you – "I am not a dime a dozen! I am Willy Loman, and you are Biff Loman!"

There is a plethora of advice columns on how to make first impressions. However, perhaps Willy Loman depicts this best in Death of a Salesman, "Walk in with a big laugh. Don't look worried. Start off with a couple of your good stories to lighten things up. It's not what you say, it's how you say it – because personality always wins the day."

Yes, personality helps but there is so much more – here is a story from Avrom that will change your perspective.

We learned earlier that after graduating from Harvard Law School, Avrom started his professional career at the Federal Trade Commission (FTC). His first assignment was to join a special taskforce that was set up to audit numerous antitrust violation settlement agreements entered by the Department of Justice (DOJ). These settlements went back many years and therefore required a thorough review of the terms of the settlement agreement and associated compliance. Avrom was puzzled as to why a particular settlement agreement was drafted in such an obscure and convoluted way. After much contemplation, he realized there was a drafting error and surprisingly the settlement agreement permitted what was intended to be prohibited.

Avrom, after telling his superior, Mr. C, about the mistake was lectured about his presumptiveness. He said to Avrom, "Who do you think you are, kid? This agreement was signed off by the highest levels in the DOJ and by the Court, do you really think they were all wrong?" Avrom politely, but to no avail, persisted in trying to explain the error. Finally, after much frustration, Avrom took a different approach. He pointed out how the agreement employed multiple negatives in the drafting. He broke the complex settlement agreement into simplified components and explained the drafting as an algebra equation. Mr. C got it! He said, "Avrom you are a genius, let's call up those pretentious lawyers in the DOJ and have some fun with them."

From that moment on, Avrom was 'the chosen one' and the genius label remained. It lasted because he treated every interaction as a first impression. He did this because he knew that one of the great mysteries of life is that desires change unexplainably – tastes in art, entertainment, and fashion. It is no different with bosses, clients, and customers. The courting doesn't stop when you get married! We need to bring the same enthusiasm, urgency, and desire as if it were the first impression.

Don't rest on your laurels.

But here's the rub: this lesson from Avrom will not change you unless you deeply internalize it. Perhaps the best fuel for this is through the limitless power of gratitude. It starts with being mindful of all the good that is done to you. The impetus of the first impression is likely because someone did you a kindness – gave you a job, purchased your services, or helped you on a team project. And what better currency to repay our indebtedness in the world than waking up each day and continuously stretching ourselves to contribute in ways others cannot. In short, again, treating every encounter as if it were the first impression.

Will Rogers joked, "You never get a second chance to make a first impression." He was right, but it all gets that much easier when the power of gratitude helps you remember that each interaction is of supreme importance.

CHAPTER 4 – MR. MARSHMALLOW

Rodney Dangerfield quipped on his secret to marriage, "We sleep in separate rooms, we have dinner apart, we take separate vacations – we're doing everything we can to keep our marriage together." This may work, but certainly is not the ingredients for a healthy marriage.

Unlike Mr. Dangerfield, Avrom and his late wife, Sarah, enjoyed each other's company. They had a long, happy, and successful marriage. This was partly due to Avrom's appreciation of Sarah's difficult childhood. Sarah was born in Poland in the 1930's. Her family barely escaped the horrors of the Holocaust by seeking refuge in Shanghai. For the duration of World War II, along with other Jewish refugees, they lived in a small, crowded ghetto, with limited food.

Throughout Avrom and Sarah's marriage, they enjoyed hosting numerous guests for Sabbath meals. The table was always beautifully decorated and overflowing with food – sixteen different salads, three types of chicken, kugels, etc.

Although Sarah and Avrom's mother had a deep and loving relationship, the abundance of food was a touchy subject. His mother thought it was wasteful and unnecessary.

"Avrom, why does she make sixteen salads and is always entertaining, I don't understand?" "Mother, she was a refugee, hungry most of the time – guests and excess food gives her comfort." "I don't like it; can't you control your wife?" "She's not my daughter; Sarah is my wife, and a husband shouldn't control his wife, he should support her." "Well, you know what you are, you are a big marshmallow!" And for many years after that, anytime Avrom's mother complained, he would pitifully say, "What can I do, I am just a big marshmallow?"

We often find ourselves in the impossible situation of having to please many people. When faced with this predicament, some are paralyzed by indecision while others seem to coast through. The secret to avoiding this predicament is setting clear goals in all areas of life. Avrom honored and loved his mother and did not want to disappoint her but, early in his marriage, he determined that Sarah and her happiness was his top priority.

Here's the lesson – when we are stuck in a situation and don't know what to do, it is likely because we don't have clear goals. Goals make decision making easy by clarifying what is and what is not important. They guide us in determining what we are willing to sacrifice and they anchor us against criticism. And, when necessary, they even allow us to be marshmallows.

The insight here is that goals extend beyond professional desires; they apply in all areas of our life. Once we have them, decision making is easy. Clarity begets decisiveness. As Benjamin Mays wisely said, "It must be borne in mind that the tragedy of life doesn't lie in not reaching your goal. The tragedy lies in having no goals to reach."

CHAPTER 5 – POSH EMPATHY!

ATTENTION, not time, is our most limited resource. Everyone is fighting for it – social media, smartphones, work, family, and personal interests. Sadly, the fallout, is the short supply of empathy.

In the early 70's, Avrom worked for the Office of Foreign Direct Investments (OFDI). As the OFDI regulated the flow of cash out of the U.S., it had outsized global importance. Avrom reported to Mr. P, the head of the agency and a worldly, sophisticated former European banker.

Mr. P invited Avrom to accompany him on a business trip to meet with top London banks in discussions related to U.S. and UK banking matters. Unfortunately, when they arrived in London, they discovered that the airline had lost Avrom's suitcase containing his phylacteries/ tefillin (religious object worn by Jewish men during morning prayer). Avrom was deeply disturbed by this as he had never missed a day praying with his tefillin.

At the first meeting of the day, he was overwhelmed by the regality of the bank office, the elaborate board room, and the nobility and deliberateness of the senior bank officials. He tried his best to focus on the meeting and conceal his inner turmoil regarding the tefillin.

During a break, the head of the bank came over and whispered, "Mr. Avrom, I consider myself a very good judge of character and I can tell that something is greatly disturbing you." Avrom graciously attempted in vain to convince him that everything was fine. "Mr. Avrom, I want to assure you that the resources of this bank are absolutely unlimited, there isn't anything we can't do." Avrom replied, "Well, unfortunately, I think there might be something you can't do!" He then explained how the airline lost his tefillin and how wearing them was necessary for prayer. "Not a problem, we are on it." At the end of the meeting, the banker again whispered to Avrom, "I have good news for you, we were able to procure a pair of tefillin." He handed Avrom the tefillin and wished him well. Avrom thanked him; he was so grateful for the herculean effort it must have taken to find a pair of tefillin.

The banker was a remarkable person – few people have the sensitivity to notice when someone is in distress, nor do they have the courage to discreetly ask the person about it and then to act. The banker had total confidence in himself and the bank to deliver.

Here's the lesson – even if we are not leaders of banks with unlimited resources, we must appreciate there is so much we can do. The first step is for us to be aware of the needs of others and then to practice empathy. Next, we need to never doubt our ability to help; we must ignore our inner voice that says, "Who am I or what can I do?" Lastly, we need to confidently act by realizing we each have unique talents that are far greater than we appreciate.

Adopting this attitude brings such richness, excitement, and limitlessness to everyday encounters. Be mindful of those around and you will be surprised what you notice and can do. As Maya Angelou brilliantly said, "I think we all have empathy. We may not have enough courage to display it."

CHAPTER 6 – I DON'T HAVE TIME...

"In my opinion, we don't devote nearly enough scientific research to finding a cure for jerks." Bill Watterson

AVROM WAS fortunate to attend Harvard Law School. During the early days of his first year, he was studying in the huge school library. He needed to read a court opinion from a California Appeals Courts, but could not locate the area in the library where he would find the case.

Avrom approached a third-year law student for his assistance in locating the needed volumes. "Excuse me but this is my first time in the library, can you direct me to where I could find this court option?" The third-year student responded, "Yes, I can, but I don't have time." And with that, he walked off. Avrom was completely stunned. How much time would it have taken this student to indicate the room where the needed volumes were located? He could have simply pointed Avrom in the right direction.

Avrom learned several things:

Some people are simply not kind.

Creating an environment in which constant study becomes an obsessive ritual can go too far.

There should never be a situation where you can't spare a few seconds to help someone out.

Never let yourself become so engrossed with a project that you are unwilling to perform a simple act of kindness.

"I don't have time to help you" is virtually the same as "I don't want to help you."

Certainly, few of us act as rudely and insensitively as the Harvard law student who was truly a jerk to Avrom. However, at times, we don't realize that something seemingly small can be urgent to another person. It could be as insignificant as responding to an email, making a connection, or giving information. Whatever it may be, a small effort can go a long way.

Next time you find yourself saying, "I don't have time", replace it with "I don't want." It is painful to realize because only a jerk would say that!

CHAPTER 7 – YOU NEVER KNOW...

A JOY OF LIFE is you never know who you will meet, why you met them, and when you will meet them again. And, of course, we should be kind to everyone because it is the right thing to do. But, we should also be kind because you just really never know....

Avrom loves people and regardless of whom he meets he engages them in conversation. Many years ago, he hired a driver, Sol, to take him to the airport. The driver told him an incredible story about his wife, Shirley. Sol fell in love and took his fiancé, Shirley, to meet his parents for the first time. When the young couple arrived at his parents' home, his mother reacted as Sol had expected, showing Shirley much affection. But, surprisingly, his father was uncharacteristically reserved. And, to add to the awkwardness, Shirley also seemed uncomfortable meeting her future father-in-law.

Later that evening, Shirley explained her strange behavior to Sol. Some years earlier, she was employed as a receptionist in a doctor's office. A man arrived for his appointment, checked in, sat down in the waiting room, and lit up a large cigar. Shirley called out to him that cigar smoking was not permitted. The patient ignored her. Shirley repeated her statement in a louder tone. He still ignored her. Finally, she shouted that if he didn't put out the cigar immediately, she would put it out for him. He continued to ignore her. She got up, went to the patient, grabbed the cigar from his mouth, threw it on the floor, and smashed it.

You guessed it: the patient turned out to be Shirley's prospective father-in-law. Sol told Avrom that, unfortunately, his wife and father over the many years they knew each other never developed an easy relationship.

This ironic story is a great example of 'you just never know'. And you can never assume that your behavior will be forgotten. In this case, the extreme behavior with a stranger led to an awkward, uncomfortable, and yet unavoidable relationship.

Avrom has counseled thousands of people on how to remove unnecessary walls between family and friends. It starts with recognizing that it is possible to forgive past sins, slights, or misunderstandings. Next, attempt to repair personal ill-feeling by expressing regret for earlier behavior. Once this is complete, agree to adjust your behavior to get along.

And if this doesn't work, Avrom advises humor to turn an embarrassment into a funny comment. Imagine their relationship if Shirley would have brought her father-in-law an expensive cigar at their next visit.

CHAPTER 10 – CALL ME AVROM...

WHEN WE REflect on extraordinary people, it is not what they did that we remember, rather, it is how they made us feel and how they inspired us to be better.

For seven years, during the 1980s, Avrom served as Deputy Special Counsel at the U.S. Department of Energy, enforcing crude oil price regulations against the 34 largest U.S. oil companies. In the course of this work, Avrom became acquainted with many senior oil company executives and with senior attorneys from prominent national law firms. He made it a standard practice to treat everyone cordially, kindly, and respectfully, even when engaged in contentious disputes.

Near the end of his tenure as a government official, Avrom received a phone call from a senior partner of a large law firm (Mr. G) who represented a huge oil company that had had many legal battles with the DOE. "Avrom, I would like to speak with you about something that would not be an appropriate subject in a government building. Can we meet for coffee?"

Avrom was surprised by the request and with curiosity agreed to the meeting. He felt assured of its legitimacy since Mr. G had a splendid record of personal integrity. Avrom could not figure out what subject Mr. G had in mind and why he felt the need to meet at a neutral site.

The day of the meeting arrived; Avrom and Mr. G greeted each other warmly and exchanged pleasantries. Finally, Avrom would find out the reason for the meeting. Mr. G told Avrom that he was not Jewish but was married to a Jewish woman and their children were being brought up in her faith. His son was preparing for his Bar Mitzvah, a coming-of-age ritual for a 13-year-old boy, and the couple had met with the rabbi where the ceremony would be held. The rabbi had suggested that Mr. G take a Hebrew name just for the day of the Bar Mitzvah and offered some choices. Mr. G told Avrom that he had explained to the rabbi that his selection for a name was Avrom, the man he most respected and the one he would like his son most to emulate. Mr. G continued saying that had been so impressed by Avrom's conduct over the many years of their relationship that it would be a great honor to be called Avrom, if only for a day. Avrom was humbled by these words and so appreciative to be thought of so respectfully.

We can never know how strong an affect our personal behavior and conduct can have on others. As Jackie Robinson said, "A life is not important except in the impact it has on other lives."

CONCLUSION

In 2019, after much beseeching, Avrom agreed to be honored at a community event. Hundreds of people came from around the world and shared stories of how Avrom bettered their lives. When it came time for Avrom to speak, everyone was at the edge of their seat, eagerly awaiting his wisdom. "In anticipation of this occasion, I was seized with two great fears. The first one was the fear of considering how many fantastic achievements I have made that some of them would be omitted. The second fear I had, is even worse, that the magnitude of my contributions would be exaggerated. Thank God it didn't happen." The room erupted in laughter.

Of course, I will never have Avrom's wit, wisdom, scholarship, or stellar character. But, thanks to my visits, I have something to aspire to. As a tax lawyer, I spend most of my day trying to perfect the mastery of complex tax rules around the world. This is important for my professional development. However, I have learned from Avrom that I need to invest an equal amount of energy in my personal development.

The Chazon Ish, a great 19th century rabbi, taught, "It requires extra caution to make the main thing, into the main thing." The main thing isn't complicated when we have clear priorities. But, as Harold Macmillan, the British statesman and former Prime Minister, when asked what was most likely to send his government work off course, said, "Events, dear boy, events".

In Leidy Klotz's book, *Subtract*, he explains how subtraction is an overlooked force for change and powerful tool to remove the constraining forces clouding the "main thing." When we cut out the unnecessary in life and remove the walls holding us back, we will find there is plenty of space for what is important and meaningful.

Avrom applied subtraction and found the time daily to invest in perfecting his wit, the depth of his wisdom and scholarship, and the refinement of his character.

As you continue the journey of your life, I hope this book helps clarify your priorities, gives you the tools to avoid any unnecessary "events", and the insights to improve your life. It will not make you become Avrom, but I hope it will help you become the person you are meant to be, YOU. And this is the "main thing!"

Avrom as a child

This is the picture of Avrom that fell
out of Sarah's locker

Checkmate!

Avrom and Sarah's wedding

Avrom's parents

Avrom and Sarah with his family

Avrom's grandfather, "I will not even look"

Avrom's children

Avrom at work

Avrom with the author's son Ezra

The author with Avrom on a Wednesday visit

Printed in Great Britain
by Amazon